IT Across the Primary Curriculum

EDITED BY
Rob Crompton
Philip Mann

CASSELL

Dedicated to Chris M. Robinson in recognition
of her contribution to IT and to education

Cassell
Wellington House
125 Strand
London WC2R 0BB

127 West 24th Street
New York
NY 10011

First published 1996

British Library Cataloguing-in-Publication Data
A catalogue record for this book is available from the British Library.

ISBN 0-304-33288-7 (hardback)
       0-304-33290-9 (paperback)

Designed and Typeset by Ben Cracknell Studios

Printed and bound in Singapore by Kyodo Printing Co. PTE Ltd

Contents

Contributors iv

Preface vii

Acknowledgements viii

1 The Educational Context 1
Rob Crompton and Philip Mann

2 Opportunities 12
Rob Crompton and Philip Mann

3 Communicating Information: Words 20
Rob Crompton and Philip Mann

4 Communicating Information: Art 36
Ged Gast

5 Communicating Information: Music 59
David Congdon

6 Handling Information 70
Colin Rouse and Philip Mann

7 Modelling 85
Chris Salt

8 Control and Monitoring 100
Philip Mann and Rob Crompton

9 Assessing IT 108
Janice Staines and Rob Crompton

10 Towards a School IT Policy 118
Jenny Short

11 Initial Training and Staff Development 128
Rob Crompton and Philip Mann

12 Trends in Educational IT 141
Philip Mann and Rob Crompton

Index 149

Contributors

David Congdon
David initially taught music in a middle school before becoming a class teacher in a large primary school. During this time he was a member of a team which trained teachers in the use of IT and subsequently became an advisory teacher for music and a Key Stage 1 moderator. His present post is music inspector, which involves advisory and curriculum development work as well as OFSTED primary and secondary inspections. David has contributed to a previous book on IT in the primary classroom and to many professional journals. He has been the keynote speaker and course tutor at a number of national conferences. A consummate musician, David has had several musicals published and is the author of a very popular educational music software package.

Rob Crompton
Rob has taught across the whole age range in primary schools and has been the headteacher of a village school in Cambridgeshire and a large primary school in Berkshire. He is a lecturer in primary education at the University of Reading where he leads the PGCE Early Years course and is associate director of the BA(Ed) course. As a Registered Inspector with OFSTED he visits schools throughout the country and values the opportunity to support the development of good primary practice. In addition to consultancy work in information technology, mathematics and school management, Rob has written scripts for children's television and articles in professional journals, as well as composing musicals and songs.

Ged Gast
Ged trained in fine art and holds an honours degree from Wolverhampton Polytechnic. His major study was in sculpture; his subsidiary interests included film, photography and sound. After taking his PGCE in art education he initially taught art and ceramics in a secondary school. He developed an early interest in the role of computers in art education and, as head of a successful art

department, was invited to contribute to an LEA project focusing on this issue. After a two-year secondment to Berkshire's IT support team he became an advisory teacher for art and subsequently took up his current post as art advisor. In addition to taking part in OFSTED inspections he provides consultancy, training and support for teachers in the use of IT in art and design across all school phases.

Philip Mann

Philip graduated from Edinburgh University with degrees in Physics and Psychology. He started teaching in London and has worked for Berkshire LEA for 17 years, moving from deputy headship of a primary school to headship then to advisory teacher for information technology. He has helped to run IT in-service training in the county for eleven years. Additional responsibilities have included moderation of assessment, OFSTED inspections and liaison work. He has worked in close co-operation with Reading University in the provision of IT training for a number of years.

Colin Rouse

Colin is the deputy headteacher of Cranbourne Primary School in Winkfield, Berkshire. He is known for his work in IT and has provided INSET on a variety of IT activities. He has produced educational support materials for leading software houses and has written many articles for national computer magazines and journals. As a member of the British Computer Society's Education National Working Party he is looking at the quality of teaching and learning in IT and is also involved in the evaluation of the use of CD-ROM in primary classrooms.

Chris Salt

Chris is the General Advisor for Design Technology and Information Technology for the London borough of Houndslow. In the early 1970s he started teaching design technology and more recently extended his brief to include IT. Following a period as Head of Technology and IT Co-ordinator at Sandhurst School, he became an advisory teacher working with teachers to support the development of IT within the early years, primary and secondary curriculum. Chris has run accredited courses in IT through the University of Reading and is currently external examiner for the PGCE course at Brunel University. As an OFSTED inspector he has reported on IT at all key stages and in special schools.

Jenny Short

Jenny trained originally as a specialist PE teacher and taught in schools ranging from large comprehensives to small village primaries. After living in Tulsa, Oklahoma for a time she returned to the UK to find that computers had arrived in schools. Since then a developing interest in IT has led Jenny to co-ordination roles in all schools in which she has taught and an involvement in in-service training. She is currently headteacher of a junior school and is still actively involved in PE. Jenny has contributed to educational publications and has recently completed an MA in primary education.

Janice Staines

Janice was a primary teacher with Walsall LEA for 14 years. During this time she developed an interest in IT when taking part in the Walsall Logo Project. She felt that the use of the computer provided insights into how children learn and her increasing expertise in this field led to her appointment as a Primary Curriculum Officer with the Micro-electronics Education Support Unit (MESU). Janice is currently a Senior Programme Officer with the National Council for Educational Technology (NCET) where one of her roles is to provide support and guidance for primary advisory teachers, class teachers and teacher educators in the use of IT to support the primary curriculum.

Preface

There can be few areas in human knowledge and understanding which have undergone such dramatic change as information technology. With breathtaking speed this technology has influenced most areas of society, including educational thinking and practice.

This book is intended to inform anyone concerned with the educational process, particularly at primary level. It is hoped that it will serve to illustrate the change in classroom practice brought about by information technology, and it has been written with teachers and parents in mind. Additionally it provides a rich source of material for anyone involved in educational training, advisory work and school inspection.

New areas of knowledge often require new vocabularies. In the field of information technology the accompanying jargon has often been a barrier to those lacking in confidence. This book tries to describe current practice in a jargon-free manner. Inevitably certain words and phrases may be new to the reader. However, in a short time, vocabulary can become part of everyday speech. The National Curriculum begat new terms such as ATs, PoS, KS1 and Levels of Attainment which, despite initial resistance, have become essential to the educational process.

The chapters in this book can stand alone and, following the introduction, they need not be read in any particular sequence.

Rob Crompton and Philip Mann

Acknowledgements

The authors would like to acknowledge the help received from the many people who have made this book possible. In addition to the contributors many colleagues have given informal help and advice. In particular we wish to acknowledge the encouragement and generous support given by Chris Robson. Chris died as this book was going to press. She was a very special friend and highly professional colleague whose enthusiasm and commitment influenced the development of IT both in the UK and abroad.

Our aim of making the book as attractive and accessible as possible has been greatly helped by the cartoons of Peter Dixon and through the assistance received from the technical support staff at both the University of Reading and the Berkshire Information Technology Centre in reproducing children's work. All the photographs were taken by the editors, with the exception of those of children working with the Roamer, which were taken by Amanda Champ.

Our main source of inspiration has of course been the children with whom we have worked and the teachers who continue to find creative ways of introducing information technology into their teaching across the curriculum. Our grateful thanks to the teachers and children of the following schools who have allowed us to celebrate their achievements and to reproduce their work:

Alfred Sutton Primary, Reading
Aldryngton Primary, Earley
Coombes Infant, Arborfield
Cranbourne Primary, Windsor
Crown Wood Primary, Bracknell
Garland Junior, Mortimer
John Rankin Infant, Newbury
Oxford Road Primary, Reading
Palmer Junior, Wokingham
St Martin's RC Primary, Caversham
Wildridings Primary, Bracknell
Wellington Primary, Somerset

The Educational Context

THE NATIONAL CURRICULUM

There can be little doubt that the introduction of the National Curriculum has been a major influence on the way teachers think about and organize their approach to children's learning in schools. Less than a decade ago the idea of a national curriculum was an anathema to the majority of primary teachers, and some 80,000 negative responses were made to the government's original consultative document. However, despite some serious problems in terms of assessment and the construction of league tables, and even before the reforms proposed by the Dearing Report, opinion seems to have dramatically changed to one of support. Certainly the principle of a national framework for the curriculum has been widely accepted. The notion of a minimum entitlement which is not dependent on the individual interests and enthusiasms of teachers, nor on the particular bandwagon of the headteacher or local authority adviser, has obvious advantages. Although the National Curriculum orders were increasingly prescriptive, within the framework teachers were in theory free to adopt their own approach. How realistic was this freedom?

Primary practice

Reports made by OFSTED inspectors must identify key issues for action which are derived from the close scrutiny of all aspects of the school's life. An informal survey of such reports indicates that many schools are asked to seek ways in which the curriculum could be differentiated to meet the needs of children across a wide ability range. Although matching and differentiation were major concerns of HMI in pre-National Curriculum days, the introduction of central control, with the accompanying plethora of programmes, targets and levels does not appear to have helped teachers to provide suitably differentiated learning experiences for their children. Indeed it could be argued that the pursuit of the ubiquitous tick on the record sheet has been counterproductive in this respect. Many teachers in an effort to cover or 'visit' attainment targets have resorted to an almost continuous stream of worksheets accompanied by the use of published schemes for many of the core and foundation subjects. The first 'death by worksheet' has yet to be recorded, but the fact that such a phrase has become part of everyday vocabulary must be significant. This is not to decry in any way the efforts of teachers in classrooms. The construction of a curriculum with such closely defined content, and with an almost ludicrous recording and reporting regime, made a concentration on content and a diminishing attention to process almost inevitable. Thus the freedom of teachers to adopt methods in which they fundamentally believed was severely restricted. There were notable exceptions to this when individual teachers and often whole schools were sufficiently creative – and had the necessary energy – to provide an alternative approach which met the demands of the National Curriculum in ways which were more in keeping with their practical understanding of how children learn.

Advice for teachers

Recognizing the difficulties faced by teachers in meeting the new demands, attempts were made during the life of the original curriculum orders to help them in the organization and management of their classrooms. The discussion paper *Curriculum Organisation and Classroom Practice in Primary Schools* (1992), known as the 'three wise men report', discussed the importance of using a variety of groupings – whole class, small groups and individual – and this perhaps helped some teachers to adopt appropriate strategies without the residual 'guilt' which is often apparent when teachers apologize to advisers, university tutors and other visitors for teaching the whole class lesson! It was encouraging to note that the authors had based some of their assertions on research evidence, although there was an element of 'political correctness' which can lead to simple solutions being proffered by those with no experience of classrooms.

Other centrally produced documents were intended to be helpful but perhaps raised more questions rather than providing answers. For example *Primary Matters* (1994), a survey by OFSTED which reported on the practice in 49 primary schools contained some rather tautologous statements. In offering advice to general medical practitioners we would probably suggest that they: keep up to date with clinical treatments, listen to their patients, identify symptoms, prescribe appropriate drugs, monitor progress and maintain careful records. This of course begs many questions and is probably not too helpful, but it is patently good advice. Teachers are informed by *Primary Matters* that success can be achieved by: having a good knowledge of the subject being taught, using good questioning skills, making effective use of exposition, instruction and direct teaching, using a good balance of grouping strategies including whole-class, small-group or individual work and using ability grouping effectively. Although the report does expand some of these points, many of the factors are fairly obvious to teachers who have been searching for effective strategies for many years. For example, what exactly constitutes effective use of exposition, instruction and direct teaching; and are certain methods better for particular age groups or curriculum areas?

The Dearing reforms

In response to the overwhelming tide of opinion, one of the main aims of the Dearing Committee was to return to teachers a substantial amount of time in which they could respond to particular circumstances, providing for individual needs and developing the interests and talents of their children. Whilst there is some debate about the content of the revised orders, the simplification of the Programmes of Study and the adoption of level descriptions as opposed to highly complicated levels of attainment have been widely welcomed. This together with the moratorium on further changes offers an opportunity for teachers to provide a rich curriculum which both meets legal requirements and involves their children in exciting and stimulating learning experiences. How can Information Technology assist in this process? This book aims to help teachers see the role that IT can play in pursuit of this aim.

IT AND THE PRIMARY CURRICULUM

Second only to the impact of the National Curriculum which is discussed above, it is likely that most people would identify the introduction of technology, and in particular Information Technology, as the next most significant change in primary classrooms. This was perhaps inevitable given the exponential growth of IT generally, although this does not explain the high regard in which the UK is held throughout the world in the use of computers in primary schools.

Centrally-funded activities such as the MEP (Microcomputers in Education Programme), the MESU (Microcomputers in Education Support Group) and more recently the NCET (National Council for Educational Technology) have exerted a great influence. These organizations have consistently attracted personnel who are educationalists first and technologists second. Central to their work therefore was the need to provide support for a broad and balanced curriculum; the involvement of IT was to enhance and enrich the children's experience whilst concurrently developing generic IT skills. This was in marked contrast to the approach taken in other countries where the emphasis initially was heavily placed on the use of IT to increase knowledge, focusing on content rather than concepts and process.

During this pioneering period LEAs (Local Education Authorities) held a much higher proportion of funds centrally than was possible following the introduction of LMS (Local Management of Schools). Most authorities were able to establish teams of advisers and advisory teachers whose influence was very significant. Teachers in schools needed such personal support. It is probably possible, for example, to develop expertise in teaching mathematics by reading widely on the subject. Information Technology, however, requires a degree of practical skill which can only realistically be provided through personal teaching rather than distance learning, and anyone who has struggled through a computer manual will appreciate the efficiency and effectiveness of personal support. Throughout the country, teachers were able to attend a variety of in-service courses which were invaluable in disseminating ideas and developing practical expertise and confidence. The cross-fertilization of ideas between teachers, schools and advisers in different areas was also greatly enhanced by the establishment of specialist organizations such as MAPE (Micros and Primary Education) which began to publish regular journals and to hold annual conferences.

The existence of both national and local frameworks for the dissemination of good practice and the provision of in-service training has had an enormous impact in raising IT capability in the teaching profession. The majority of teachers appear keen to use IT in their classrooms, and the demand for places on in-service courses is undiminished. However, a consequence of the increasing devolvement of funds to schools has meant that LEAs have had to reduce the number of advisory teachers for IT. Ironically central support had diminished concurrently with increasing requirements of IT in the classroom. Although a substantial amount of money is specifically targeted towards IT through the annual GEST (Grant for Educational Support and Training) budget, the training so provided has tended to be less far-reaching than earlier provision, which was characterized by a wider variety of courses. When funding was held centrally by LEAs, advisory teams could respond more effectively to local needs, providing a wide range of courses from single twilight sessions to more sustained individual school support. As mentioned above, publications are no substitute for practical experience, but in providing an overview of the current curriculum requirements and a range of examples from primary classrooms, it is hoped that this book will augment and support a variety of pre-service and in-service activities.

IT IN THE NATIONAL CURRICULUM

The status of IT in the National Curriculum has been clarified by the new orders. Indeed, although the brief for the SCAA (School Curriculum and Assessment Authority) working parties was to simplify existing Programmes of Study (without adding anything in terms of content), it could be argued that as far as IT is concerned, more is demanded by the revised orders. There is a necessity for pupils to develop their basic IT skills within all curriculum subjects with the exception of PE. When thinking about the position of IT in the curriculum, it is helpful to keep in mind the interrelationship between the two major aspects of pupils' learning: it supports the development of knowledge and understanding of subjects, and through this process IT capability is strengthened.

The orders for IT are summarized in figures 1.1 and 1.2.

THE CHALLENGE OF IT

How can schools and individual teachers ensure that they are providing their pupils with their full 'entitlement' to IT? Significant progress has been made in three main areas which can help teachers to fulfil this aim.

The new orders

In many ways the new curriculum orders provide a useful conceptual framework within which to analyse IT provision. Each programme of study has three sections:

1. Opportunities pupils should be given
2. Communicating and handling information
3. Controlling, monitoring and modelling

And although in practice such finite distinctions are often inappropriate, these headings can be very helpful when planning, monitoring and assessing information technology. These three headings should be central to a school's policy for IT. This is further discussed in chapter 10.

Information Technology: Programmes of study

PROGRAMMES OF STUDY	Key Stage 1	Key Stage 2
	Pupils should be given opportunities to: **a** Use a variety of IT equipment and software, including microcomputers and various keyboards, to carry out a variety of functions in a range of contexts; **b** explore the use of computer systems and control technology in everyday life; **c** examine and discuss their experiences of IT and look at the use of IT in the outside world.	Pupils should be given opportunities to: **a** use IT to explore and solve problems in the context of work across a variety of subjects; **b** use IT to further their understanding of information that they have retrieved and processed; **c** discuss their experiences of using IT and assess its value in their working practices; **d** investigate parallels with the use of IT in the wider world, consider the effects of such uses and compare them with other methods.
	Communicating and handling information Pupils should be taught to: **a** generate and communicate their ideas in different forms, using text, tables, pictures and sound; **b** enter and store information; **c** retrieve, process and display information that has been stored.	**Communicating and handling information** Pupils should be taught to: **a** use IT equipment and software to communicate ideas and information in a variety of forms, incorporating text, graphics, pictures and sound, as appropriate, showing sensitivity to the needs of their audience; **b** use IT equipment and software to organize, reorganize and analyze ideas and information; **c** select suitable information and media and classify and prepare information for processing with IT, checking for accuracy; **d** interpret, analyse and check the plausibility of information held on IT systems and select the elements required for particular purposes, considering the consequences of any errors.
	Controlling and modelling Pupils should be taught to: **a** recognize that control is integral to many everyday devices; **b** give direct signals or commands that produce a variety of outcomes and describe the effects of their actions; **c** use IT-based models or simulations to explore aspects of real and imaginary situations.	**Controlling, monitoring and modelling** Pupils should be taught to: **a** create, test, modify and store sequences of instructions to control events; **b** use IT equipment and software to monitor external events; **c** explore the effect of changing variables in simulations and similar packages, to ask and answer questions of the 'What would happen if. . .?' type; **d** recognize patterns and relationships in the results obtained from IT-based models or simulations, predicting the outcomes of different decisions that could be made.

Figure 1.1

Information Technology: Level descriptions

Level 1

Pupils use IT to assemble text and symbols to help them communicate ideas. They explore information held on IT systems showing an awareness that information exists in a variety of forms. They recognize that many everyday devices respond to signals and commands, and that they can select options when using such devices to produce different outcomes.

Level 2

Pupils use IT to help them generate and communicate ideas in different forms, such as text, tables, pictures and sound. With some support, they retrieve and store work. They use IT to sort and classify information and to present their findings. Pupils control devices purposefully and describe the effects of their actions. They use IT-based models or simulations to investigate options as they explore aspects of real and imaginary situations.

Level 3

Pupils use IT to generate, amend, organize and present ideas. They use IT to save data and to access stored information, following straightforward lines of enquiry. They understand how to control equipment to achieve specific outcomes by giving a series of instructions. They use IT-based models or simulations to help them make decisions and are aware of the consequences of their choices. They describe their use of IT and its use in the outside world.

Level 4

Pupils use IT to combine different forms of information and show an awareness of audience. They add to, amend and interrogate information that has been stored. They understand the need for care in framing questions when collecting, accessing and interrogating information. Pupils interpret their findings, question plausibility and recognise that poor quality information yields unreliable results. Pupils use IT systems to control events in a predetermined manner, to sense physical data and to display it. They use IT-based models and simulations to explore patterns and relationships and make simple predictions about the consequences of their decision-making. They compare their use of IT with other methods.

Level 5

Pupils use IT to organize, refine and present information in different forms and styles for specific purposes and audiences. They select the information needed for different purposes, check its accuracy and organize and prepare it in a form suitable for processing using IT. They create sets of instructions to control events, and are becoming sensitive to the needs for precision in framing and sequencing instructions. They explore the effects of changing the variables in a computer model. They communicate their knowledge and experience of using IT and assess its use in their working practices.

Figure 1.2

'The ease of using programs has increased'

Software

The problem of searching through countless catalogues in order to find suitable software which matched a particular computer system has largely been overcome. The number of publishers of educational software has dramatically reduced in recent years from around 120 in the mid-1980s to just a few major companies in the late-1990s. The new generation of computer systems has brought with it greater demands for technical expertise in software writing, and the 'cottage industry' approach has largely disappeared. The larger companies have the resources to devote much time and effort to researching educational possibilities and to the careful development and trialling of new software.

The trend has been away from the idea that a particular program can be produced to match every need of an individual pupil to highly sophisticated programs which can be configured to suit a range of uses. For example, the word processing programs to be found in many classrooms look very similar to those used by professional organizations, but when being used by six-year-olds, many of the more advanced facilities may have been 'hidden' by the teacher.

Although programs for children with special educational needs may still be very specific, 'content-free' applications – word processors, databases, spreadsheets, art packages – have been developed which are sufficient to meet the needs of the new National Curriculum requirements. Where programs are targeted towards a particular curriculum subject, again the tendency is to provide suggestions for a wide range of cross-curricular activity. Thus the number of different programs with which a teacher needs to be familiar can be reduced to a central core or 'toolbox', and within a school the children can use the same applications with increasing levels of sophistication.

Hardware

As the complexity of writing programs has grown, conversely the ease of using programs has increased. Whereas in the recent past one often had to start from scratch when working with a new program, skills and techniques developed

'Virtual Teaching in 2095'

with one program are increasingly transferable to another. Indeed, the universal introduction of the Windows environment has meant that skills learnt using one system are usually appropriate for other computers. Also, software has become generally less 'hardware specific'. It was frustrating for many teachers to find a useful program and to learn that it was 'only available for the BBC Master'. For this reason, this book does not look in detail at one computer system and, where specific programs and computers are mentioned, the same program may well be available in a variety of formats, and there will almost certainly be a very similar program available for a different system.

The only assumption is that one of the new generation of computers is being used. Any such statement in a book about information technology is dangerous, of course. In chapter 12 new trends are discussed and some attempt is made to predict future developments, but it is certain that between the publication of this book and the end of the five-year moratorium on curriculum change there will have been many technological innovations. It is likely, however, that the fundamental principles upon which the practical suggestions are based will remain applicable for the foreseeable future.

The opportunities still available through the use of older machines should be acknowledged here. Although the facilities offered by machines such as the BBC and the RM Nimbus are very modest by current standards, many of the requirements of the revised National Curriculum can be achieved using such systems. It is not realistic to expect schools to be able to upgrade their hardware in response to every new technological development and, unless substantial government funds are invested, the average primary school will be using some 'out-of-date' machines well into the future.

AIMS

The aims of this book are:

- to provide insight and understanding of how IT can be used;
- to support the whole curriculum, in particular the requirements of the National Curriculum;
- to clarify the term 'IT capability';
- to share the experiences of classroom teachers, providing examples of how organization and management issues can be addressed;
- to discuss ways in which a whole-school approach can support the whole curriculum and enhance the assessment and progression in IT skills;
- to offer suggestions for initial teacher education and in-service work.

STRUCTURE

Following a discussion of IT 'basic skills' and some ideas for the inclusion of IT within the subjects of the National Curriculum, the next four chapters provide practical suggestions in the area of communicating and handling information. Modelling, control and monitoring are addressed in the following two chapters and subsequently the focus of the book moves from the classroom to the whole school and more general issues. These chapters should be particularly useful to co-ordinators who are responsible for the development of IT policies and assessment, and for staff development. New trends in technology are reviewed but of course, in the field of IT the word 'new' cannot be applied to any innovation for long. Any attempt to summarize such developments is fraught with difficulty. However, should a copy of this book survive until 2094, at least it might provide our successors with much amusement!

REFERENCES

Alexander, R., Rose, J. and Woodhead, C. (1992) *Curriculum Organisation and Classroom Practice in Primary Schools.* London: DES.

Dearing, R. (1994) *The National Curriculum and its Assessment: Final Report.* London: SCAA.

DFE (1995) *Key Stages 1 and 2 of the National Curriculum (England).* London: HMSO.

OFSTED (1994) *Primary Matters: A Discussion on Teaching and Learning in Primary Schools.* London: HMSO.

Opportunities

This chapter has two main aims (1) to provide some suggestions about basic information technology skills and (2) to identify and clarify the role of IT within the subjects of the primary curriculum.

BASIC IT SKILLS

The concept of basic skills in IT is relatively new, making its first formal appearance in the Final Dearing Report:

> The distinctive purpose of Key Stage 1, which covers two years, is to lay the foundation of future learning by:
>
> i) developing the basic skills in reading, writing, speaking, listening, number and information technology...
>
> ...the distinctive purposes of the first two years [of Key Stage 2] might be described as:
>
> i) the development and consolidation of the basic skills of oracy, literacy, numeracy and information technology through a range of subject content...

All teachers have an understanding of what is meant by basic oracy, literacy and numeracy skills and, although accepting the fact that children do not necessarily develop these in a strictly hierarchical way, there would be a reasonable consensus about progression from one stage to another. Skills in IT have not been defined to the same extent. There is very little research evidence to support an intuitive feeling that some developmental sequence might exist. Which skills can be regarded as basic and which of a higher order? Is it better for children to learn how to print out a file before finding out how to retrieve data from a simple database? It is not uncommon to overhear a six-year-old saying, 'You can't print that – you haven't loaded a printer driver', whilst at the same time many teachers will be unsure of this procedure.

A further difference between the other basic skills and IT skills is of course IT's heavy dependence on expensive equipment. One of the most important tasks for teachers is to enable their pupils to develop independence. Not only is this necessary for children if they are to become autonomous learners but also, unless children have a certain level of independence, teaching would be impossible. In a typical classroom a small group of two or three children will be using the computer while the rest of the class are engaged in other activities. The greater their independence, the better able the teacher is to devote time to the whole class. Being constantly asked, 'How do we save it Miss? Why won't it work?' is a great hindrance and can lead to frustration on both sides.

Many teachers have found that a very effective way of ensuring that all pupils develop the basic skills essential for independence is to use the cascading principle. For example, a small group of perhaps four children are introduced to a particular technique such as saving and retrieving text. This might take place during lunchtime or immediately after school. After they have had some time for practice and consolidation they are asked to show a 'buddy' and the process continues until all the children are confident with the technique. Another group of children can be given the responsibility of introducing others to printing and so on. The teacher does not completely rely on this apprenticeship model of course, and carefully monitors the situation. Children usually respond very positively to this arrangement but obviously care should be taken to ensure that everyone has had a turn at being the 'expert'. Some form of self-assessment can be employed, perhaps using check sheets described in Chapter 9.

The concept of a 'spiral' curriculum is highly appropriate when considering IT skills. To take the examples mentioned above, the ability to save and retrieve text can be refined from carrying out these operations when using a very user-friendly program, to saving 'text files' as opposed to 'documents', through to saving text as an ASCII file (American Standard Code for Information Exchange, the most common way of saving text for use in different types of computer) and loading it into a quite different program on another machine. Printing from a menu is one thing whilst setting up the printer using the printer control procedure demands a higher level of understanding.

Given these cautions about defining a hierarchy, and notwithstanding the principle that each skill will be developed in relation to increased knowledge and understanding, the following two examples provide a reasonable structure for planning, assessing and recording progress in basic IT capability.

Word processing and desktop publishing

Word processing

entering text
editing text
choosing and changing fonts – type, size, colour
justifying – left, right, centre, fully
moving text
saving text
loading text
using clipboard – cut and paste
printing – whole document, pages, portrait/landscape
loading printer driver

Desktop publishing

importing graphics
designing pages – adjusting text and re-sizing graphics
selecting headings – headlines, captions
using frames – creating, adjusting, borders

Again, it should be emphasized that children are most likely to learn a new technique when they need it. For example they may be able to print work successfully before they have fully developed their editing skills. Also, the emphasis here is on IT and not on aspects of 'authoring', such as spelling, syntax, structure and a sense of audience.

Information handling

Similarly, the following suggestions are not intended to summarize the full range of information-handling skills. From their early sorting and classifying activities, children will be developing skills essential to their subsequent work with more complicated data. They will have a whole range of further experiences which are not dependent on IT but are directly related to information handling. They will have constructed three-dimensional histograms using matchboxes and will have taken turns to add their own favourite food or toy to the wall chart. From the beginning they will have been asked to draw inferences from the information and to begin to hypothesize. The following list focuses only on the mechanical skills of data handling with IT. It does not include the higher-order skills discussed in Chapter 6.

Mechanical skills

finding information from a simple frequency table – What is Robert's
    favourite food?

entering data into an existing database

generating graphs on screen – bar charts, pie charts, scattergrams

logical searching – AND/OR searches

using an existing structure to collect and analyse data

choosing and using an appropriate type of database – card index,
    binary tree, spreadsheet

presenting information appropriately – selecting the most significant
    findings and choosing text and graphical representations which
    illustrate these

Attempts to define basic IT skills perhaps serve only to indicate the underlying flaw in this approach. In the same way that listening to children read 'tree, little, milk, egg, book' does not provide any clue about how basic reading skills are used, so the ability to interrogate a database and draw attractive charts and graphs does not reveal the extent of associated thinking skills. IT is a relatively new curriculum activity and our understanding of the relationship between the knowledge, understanding, experience and skills associated with it will grow as an increasing number of practitioners refine their teaching strategies.

IT IN CURRICULUM SUBJECTS

The appearance of IT in the Common Requirements section of every Subject Order (with the exception of PE) serves to illustrate the increased status of IT as a cross-curricular component. It also acknowledges the role IT can play in enhancing learning in a wide range of subjects. The generic skills acquired in word processing and data handling are referred to in many of the subject orders, and indeed it is through work in the subjects that many such skills will be introduced and developed. With the addition of some of the more specialist techniques required for art and control applications, the whole of the requirements of the orders for IT can be met through subjects.

The sections of the orders relating to IT at Key Stages 1 and 2 are shown below and the chapters containing further discussion and practical examples are listed.

English

Key stage 1

Reading

b. Pupils should be introduced to and should read information, both in print and on screen. They should be encouraged to make use of a range of sources of information, including dictionaries, IT-based reference materials, encyclopaedias and information presented in fictional form.

Writing

b. Pupils should have opportunities to plan and review their writing, assembling and developing their ideas on paper and on screen...

Key Stage 2

Reading

1. Range b. Pupils should read and use a wide range of sources of information, including those not designed for children. The range of non-fiction should include IT-based reference materials...

2. Key Skills c. Pupils should be taught how to find information in books and computer based sources...

Writing

2. Key Skills b. Pupils should be given opportunities to plan, draft and improve their own work on paper and on screen...

Examples: Chapters 3 and 12

Science

Key Stages 1 and 2

1. Systematic enquiry

d. use IT to collect, store, retrieve and present scientific information

Examples: Chapter 6

Mathematics

Key Stage 1

Using and applying mathematics

4. Developing mathematical reasoning

b. ask questions including *'What would happen if?'* and *'Why?' e.g. considering the behaviour of a programmable toy.*

Number

1. Pupils should be given opportunities to :

f. use computer software, including a database.

Shape, space and measure

1. Pupils should be given opportunities to:

b. use IT devices, *e.g. programmable toys, turtle graphics packages.*

Understanding and using properties of position and movement

b. understand angle as a measure of turn and recognise quarter-turns, e.g. giving instructions for rotating a programmable toy; recognise right angles.

Key Stage 2

Number

1. Pupils should be given opportunities to :

b. use calculators, computers and a range of other resources as tools for exploring number structure and to enable work with realistic data.

Shape, space and measure

1. Pupils should be given opportunities to:

c. use computers to create and transform shapes.

Handling data

1. Pupils should be given opportunities to:

c. use computers as a source of interesting data, and as a tool for representing data.

2. Collecting, representing and interpreting data

b. collect and represent discrete data appropriately using graphs and diagrams, including block graphs, pictograms and line graphs; interpret a wider range of graphs and diagrams that represent data, including pie charts, using a computer where appropriate.

Using and applying mathematics

3. Communicating mathematically

b. use mathematical forms of communication, including diagrams, tables, graphs and computer print-outs.

Examples: Chapters 6, 7 and 8

Design and Technology

Key Stages 1 and 2

Although not specifically referred to in the Programmes of Study the common principles require that opportunities should be given for pupils to apply their information technology skills capability in their study of design and technology.

> Examples: Chapters 4, 7 and 8

History

Key Stage 2

Study Unit 3b: Britain since 1930
Changes in technology and transport
a. Changes in industry and transport, including the impact of new technologies, e.g. motor cars, computers, space travel.

> Examples: Chapters 3 and 12

Geography

Key Stage 1

Geographical skills
3. Pupils should be taught to:
f. use secondary sources, *e.g. pictures, photographs (including aerial photographs), books, videos, CD-ROM encyclopaedia,* to obtain information.

Key Stage 2

Geographical skills
3. Pupils should be taught to:
f. use IT to gain access to additional information sources and assist handling, classifying and presenting evidence, *e.g. recording fieldwork evidence on spreadsheets, using newspapers on CD-ROM, using word-processing and mapping packages.*

> Examples: Chapters 3, 6, 7 and 12

Music

Key Stage 1

1. Pupils should be given opportunities to:
b. make appropriate use of IT to record sounds.

Key Stage 2

1. Pupils should be given opportunities to:
b. make appropriate use of IT to explore and record sounds.

Attainment Target 1: Performing and composing

...compose music for specific purposes and use notation(s) and, where appropriate, information technology, to explore, develop and revise musical ideas.

> Examples: Chapter 5

Physical Education

Key Stages 1 and 2

Although IT is not referred to in the Programmes of Study or the common principles for PE, opportunities could be given for pupils to apply their information technology skills. For example records of progress in gymnastics, athletics and general fitness could be maintained using spreadsheets.

> Chapters 6 and 7

Religious Education

Although not a subject within the National Curriculum every school must teach RE and there are numerous ways in which IT can support this. The comparative study of world religions lends itself to the use of a database. For example, concept keyboard overlays can be used to record, store and present information about religious buildings, artifacts and ceremonies.

Also, issues of a social, moral, cultural and spiritual nature are often raised during work with adventure games and simulations.

> Concept keyboards: Chapter 3   Databases: Chapter 6
> Adventure games and simulations: Chapter 7.

Communicating Information: Words

SPEAKING AND LISTENING

It has long been an aim of education to encourage speaking and listening; more recently this has been further refined through the expectation of specific attainment targets in the National Curriculum. This aim has proved somewhat difficult to achieve. The arrangement of classroom furniture into modular groups is usually justified in terms of the opportunities this offers children to develop speaking and listening skills, but there is much research evidence to suggest that the conversations that take place in such circumstances are often unrelated to the task in hand. Therefore children may be developing speaking and listening skills but missing out on refining those skills in a more purposeful way. The introduction of a computer – whatever the software being used – appears to be a powerful influence on the nature of the interactions within a small group. The computer seems to act as a catalyst, not only helping to maintain a focus, but generating a momentum which carries the group forward.

The composition of such groups is important of course, as a balance of personalities is essential if the more confident children are not to dominate the activity. Decisions require refined judgements by teachers who know their particular children. Most teachers will be aware of the research evidence which suggests that in many situations boys appear to dominate activities of a technical nature. Over a period of time it should be possible to try out a range of grouping strategies which provide opportunities for all children in the class to develop their speaking and listening skills whilst using computers and other IT resources (Figure 3.1).

One way of generating speaking and listening around the computer is to use programs which contain no words. A classic example of this is the program *World Without Words*, an adventure game which immediately stimulates discussion. Many programs designed for use at the early stages of language

Figure 3.1 Speaking and listening

development contain very few words and promote interaction between groups of young children. Early examples of these were *Blob*, *Window*, and *Podd*. Also particularly successful in this respect is the more recent series of programs under the name *My World*. Screens are presented which can be altered by dragging graphics or text around and relocating items to more appropriate places. The teddy can be dressed, the lion can have his features rearranged and a professional-looking weather map can be generated using symbols which the children will be familiar with from television (Figures 3.2, 3.3).

In later years speaking and listening skills can be further developed using a variety of applications. As mentioned above, if children are not working individually at the computer almost any program will stimulate debate. The role of educational programs is to generate rational discussions, to promote team work and to provide opportunities for children to use language to develop and refine their thinking. Particularly effective are adventure games and simulations.

Adventure games take children into a fantasy world, frequently involving a search for treasure, and always presenting them with problems to solve. Conversations overheard when children are involved in such adventures often

Figure 3.2
'Can you dress the teddy?'

'Like this Miss?'

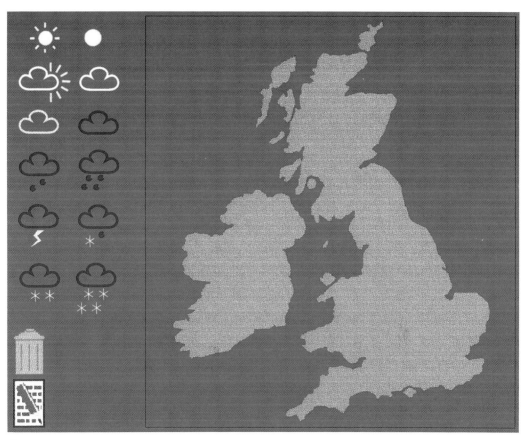

Figure 3.3
The blank weather chart
'... and the forecast for Sunday'

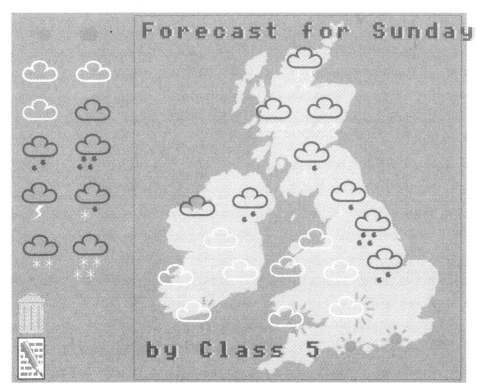

The dragon is going shopping.
What is he going to buy?
He is going to Asda to buy oranges,
chips, lollies and buns for the red,
blue, yellow and green dragons.
 The dragon wasn't very good at
pushing the trolley so he crashed
into a wall and the balloon burst.
He said "Oh dear, all my food has
got dirty and we wont be able to eat it"

Figure 3.4 Writing from Year 2 using *Granny's Garden*.

contain sentences beginning with 'What if . . .' or 'Should we try. . .' – evidence that the aims of the program are being achieved.

Similar to adventure games, but set in the real world, are simulations. Children take on the role of a detective with a crime to solve, a pilot with a journey to make or, to use a classic example, a diver who is searching for the *Mary Rose*. Simulations will also engage children in problem-solving activities and are often related to a particular subject area. For example the spoken language generated by a simulation in a historical context is likely to be somewhat different from that used in making adjustments to a Formula 1 car in preparation for a race around the Silverstone circuit.

Adventure games and simulations are examples of modelling software which is characterized by the notion of trial and error and the use of increasingly refined predictions. Chris Salt discusses this fully in Chapter 7, including the central importance of speaking and listening.

READING

Although some software contains very little text, the use of most programs involves a degree of reading. Teachers of children in the early stages of language development are usually keen to provide a classroom environment containing a wide variety of written language. Labels, notice boards, signs, timetables, interactive displays, interest tables, poems and nursery rhymes may all be used to stimulate interest in text. The computer provides a further example of text being used for particular purposes and can be a powerful stimulus for reading development.

All primary school children have grown up in a world where the use of information technology is routine, but the computer appears to have retained its power to motivate. Perhaps the fact that using a computer is seen to be such an adult activity means that it also enhances self-esteem. Whatever the reason, teachers can capitalize on children's enthusiasm by using a variety of programs where reading has a specific purpose. This is not the place to rekindle the real books vs. reading scheme debate, but in respect of computer programs the use of phonic exercises as opposed to more purposeful activities may well reduce children's motivation. This again is a decision for the individual teacher, as there may be a child who will benefit from a specific exercise which focuses on a particular skill. Such programmes need not be dull, and much success has been achieved by SEMERC (Special Educational Micro Electronics Research Centre) to produce stimulating programs for children with special educational needs.

Whilst research into the reading process continues, it is generally agreed that reading involves more than simply decoding the text. To varying degrees other strategies such as the use of contextual clues, predicting from a knowledge of common spelling patterns or the rules of syntax, play a part. For some time teachers have used the Cloze Procedure to develop reading strategies. The computer allows such tasks to be presented in a more sophisticated way with a system for recording the number of predictions used for subsequent analysis. *Developing Tray* is perhaps the best example of this.

Another technique employed by teachers in developing reading is known as DART (Directed Activities Relating to the Text). Typically this involves children focusing on the meaning and structure of a piece of text. Narrative, descriptive and functional passages can be used where children are asked to identify the most significant points, perhaps highlighting or underlining appropriate parts of the text. They may be asked to organize the passage in a different way, presenting it as a table or storyboard.

Here a modern word processing program can help enormously. The original text can be quickly transformed by the use of different fonts and colours, and the facility to cut and paste is invaluable when experimenting with the structure. In many systems text can be highlighted and simply dragged across the screen into a new location. Each attempt can be saved without losing the original version and decisions can be refined as the children become more familiar with the content. Such an application can be used by children who are just beginning to develop their critical skills, and also by more advanced students who are required to make an analytical response to a variety of texts.

The advent of the electronic encyclopaedia has made it more important for children to develop reading skills related to finding information. Their experiences in using reference books – scanning contents pages and indexes, in skimming pages for information pertinent to their enquiry – will be a great asset when searching through a CD-ROM (Compact Disc with Read Only Memory). As its name implies this compact disc can only be *read* although *read and write* CDs are being developed. The reading strategies developed using more conventional sources of information will enable children to enter an exciting new environment. For example, they can not only read about blackbirds and see a video of their flight or nest-building, but also hear their various song patterns by selecting the appropriate icon or label. Key words will be highlighted indicating that there is more information on that subject elsewhere, and children can take any picture from the screen and add it to a document of their own.

Again, the inherent motivating factor of computers is likely to prompt children to seek further information about blackbirds. Using conventional sources, and perhaps the knowledge gained from moving pictures and sound, they will be able to identify local birds. The use of CD-ROM is discussed further in Chapters 6 and 12.

Figure 3.5 'Exploring Nature' CD-ROM.

WRITING

One of the major challenges for teachers of children who are at the early stages of writing development is to find ways in which they can record their ideas on paper. Encouraged by the response made by sensitive teachers to their emergent writing many children will happily write using some familiar letters from their own names and other idiosyncratic sources and subsequently enjoy reading their stories, letters and recipes out loud. This initial enthusiasm is so important that any way of reducing the tension between content and surface features is to be welcomed. The transition from emergent to conventional writing can be helped by using the computer in a number of ways.

Figure 3.6 Street sculpture on Old Portsmouth
High Street: overlay

I met a snowman .He was wearing a bobble hat ,a woolly scarf ,mittens and a bow tie .He was made of snow. He had pieces of coal for his eyes ,a pointed carrot for his nose,a banana for his mouth .A pipe was in his mouth.He was happy because it was cold. Together we went on a sledge to a big hill,and we slid down. By Paul and Sarah.

Figure 3.7 Co-operative writing

The concept keyboard

Originally developed for children with physical disabilities, the concept keyboard enables children to select from a series of pictures, individual words and longer pieces of text by touching an overlay which has been placed on a pressure pad. This pressure pad is directly linked to the computer, and both the conventional keyboard and the concept keyboard can be used simultaneously. The overlay can contain a word/picture bank related to the class project, a series of pictures which can be placed in sequence to tell a story, jumbled sentences, and a whole variety of other supportive material.

Overlays and their associated files are constructed very easily. For example, the *Concept Designer* program enables text to be written using any suitable word processor on an Archimedes computer. This text can then be exported to the overlay file and assigned to an area of the concept keyboard. Pressing the picture of the weather-vane on the 'StrSculpts' overlay for example will result in two paragraphs of relevant text appearing on the word processor page. Children can use a combination of conventional keyboard strikes and concept keyboard presses to produce their own pieces of writing, or they might alternatively construct an overlay for other people to use, taking their own photographs and entering text onto the overlay file (Figure 3.6).

Writers' Workshop

Many teachers have adopted an approach to writing known as Writers' Workshop. Essentially this encourages children to adopt the strategies which adult writers use. Ideas are generated and discussed with friends, and a topic is chosen which typically centres around something the child is familiar with, for example a hobby, an outing or an important event. A sense of purpose is generated by identifying an audience for the writing, perhaps younger children or neighbouring schools, parents, visitors to the school and so on. A plan is made and a first draft produced and shared with a response partner who acts as proofreader and provides other feedback. The piece is then edited and modified in the light of these suggestions and the final version published in the form of an item in a class book or school magazine or in the child's personal anthology (Figures 3.7, 3.8).

The advantages of using a computer during this writing sequence are immediately obvious. Editing and redrafting can be enjoyed rather than seen as a chore, and there are numerous possibilities for publishing. Using fonts of different styles, sizes and colours together with a variety of line widths and justifications, and importing pictures and diagrams made previously with an art package, enable highly attractive publications to be produced. The value of

When Granny comes to stay

When Granny comes to stay
We all look forward to seeing her
We put flowers in the room
Rush around with the vacum cleaner
Wait excitedly for her car or the bus
to come
Here she is
Big hugs and kisses
All wrinkles and smiles
Happy to see us
What a lovely weekend
She brings us presents and sweets
Takes us to the park
Plays games with us
Loves us
We're sad when it's time for her to go
But happy that we've had a lovely time

A poem written by
Jason, Victoria, Chloe, Lucy,
Aaron, Lee

Figure 3.8 Scripts from writers' workshop

My dream time story   Crocodile Dreaming.

I am an Aboriginol. I live in the Olglas near Uluru.
I am a member of Ya clan.

Oneday I left Ya clan and went on a long journey and just
managed to cross a River with my life. And so I carried
on with my journey. I set up a camp in the out-back,
played a few notes on the didga-re-do and went to sleep.
   I woke at sun-rise and went Hunting and came back
with an emu. Then I carried on whith my journey. I had to
cross another River [luckily an empty one which is called
a creek] then I continued my journey back to Ya clan.

       Shaun Wilson

Figure 3.9 'Let's delete that bit'

When I went to Beaulieu I saw a man riding a,penny farthing bike.

I have got twin sisters called Poppy and Grace. We play in the toy kitchen together and we draw together. They are three. They are soon going to go to playgroup.

Figure 3.10 Early stages in desktop publishing

I can do running and roller-skating.
I have brown eyes.
I can write.
I can tell the time.
I can climb.
I go to St. Martin's school.

BY JENNIFER L.

My sister.

My sister is four. She goes to playgroup. She comes home for lunch. I love my sister. She plays on her own when I'm at school. She has brown hair.

Figure 3.10 (Cont'd)   Early stages in desktop publishing

such publications in terms of developing critical review and increasing motivation and self-esteem is extremely high.

Most word processors have an built-in dictionary and thesaurus which can promote independent learning, encouraging children to experiment with new words. A visit to the school office to see the secretary using very similar facilities can also motivate children to take full advantage of their time when using the computer. Ways in which children can be given increased access to word processing programs are discussed in Chapter 12.

Desktop publishing

The increasing sophistication of word processors, with facilities for adding colour and pictures to text, means that the distinction between word processing and desktop publishing is harder to make. Indeed all the requirements of the National Curriculum with respect to writing can be met using a comparatively simple word processing programme. Desktop publishing (DTP) packages are

THE SCHOOL MAIL

Date 28.9
volume 01   32p

STILL SWIMMING

Palmer Junior school are still swimming thanks to Mr Ranger and Mrs Durrant. They worked very hard all summer holidays Mrs durrent painted the walls. Mr Ranger cleaned up the changing rooms and made them plesant to go in. He has also made some benches to sit on when you are wating to get in or you can leave your towles on them

Lucky palmer school

Pritt super school visit Again!!!
This year (1994) we are very privileged to have Todd Bennet come and visit our school.   Todd Bennet is famous for running and is one of the countrys top athletes.
During his visit Todd Bennet will help Palmer pupils to do star jumps sit ups press ups and squat thrusts.These efforts will be sponsored byparents neighbours and relatives. All money collected will go towards more advents for the children of palmer. The final out come for the chidren will be a photograph with Todd Bennet A great way to end a good morning.
Editor Laura Reed.

Disaster on the railway station

There is disaster on the raiway station because some men are going to take the wokingham railways level crossings down and are going to be replaced with new ones some people think that is good but some think it is a great same.But all is not lost because they have been taken to the *national railway station!*

when you are in the pool. He has also made it a lot warmer to go in. We are swimming in september for the first time in September thanks to Ranger and Mrs Durrant.

Figure 3.11a
Desktop publishing at Key Stage 2.

used widely in primary schools, and can certainly enhance the work of those children whose IT skills are well developed.

DTP offers an enhanced capability to move text and images (Figure 3.11a, b). A variety of borders is available, and text, pictures and other graphics can be resized and rotated very easily on screen. Articles and extended stories can be structured using the pagination, indexing and master page tools. These advanced facilities sharpen the focus on design and audience and can be used in a variety of curriculum contexts.

Using DTP packages which employ exactly the same techniques as those used by professional publishers, children can produce newspapers, magazines, helpsheets, brochures, data collection sheets, labels, letter headings, tickets, programmes, and timetables which are of high quality. In replicating professional processes and increasing their own IT capabilities they can develop an understanding of the power of communication in shaping opinion and can begin to look at newspaper articles and advertisements with a more critical eye. As David Congdon suggests in relation to music in Chapter 5, work at this level will not necessarily be relevant to all children, but the pursuit of such activities in extracurricular clubs can have a beneficial effect on the use of IT throughout the school.

Electronic communication

Teletext

In addition to conventional media, writing is also increasingly generated for reproduction in electronic forms. Whilst this is probably more the concern of the secondary phase, some useful work can be done using simple teletext emulators. Children very much enjoy producing their own news bulletins for 'broadcast' to other classes. Again, they must consider the audience and use a style and vocabulary which are appropriate to the medium. Children can become rather blasé about using teletext at home, and activities which simulate a busy newsroom can certainly lead to an appreciation of the technology and human effort involved.

Electronic mail

A major innovation during recent years has been the introduction of the information superhighway. Although the total replacement of conventional postal communication by this electronic substitute may be a little way off, for the children in primary schools today the use of such technology may be commonplace when they reach adulthood. Of course primary teachers cannot anticipate the rate of change, but when thinking about developing children's writing skills it is useful to bear in mind that word processing is likely to become as ubiquitous in everyday life as it is in more formal pursuits. Until a

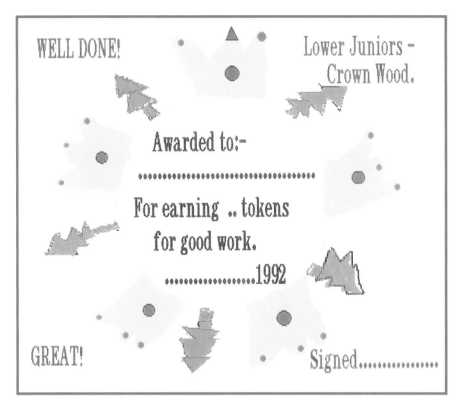

Figure 3.11b Desktop publishing at Key Stage 2

voice-activated system becomes as efficient as a mechanical interface keyboard skills will be essential. Some primary schools have already been connected to the worldwide Internet system, which takes the concept of having an audience well beyond writing in exercise books for the teacher to mark. Knowing that one's writing could be read by a potential audience of millions is quite likely to concentrate the mind!

HANDWRITING

Common sense suggests that working with a computer is not likely to have a beneficial effect on the development of handwriting. However, as discussed above, the motivational factor in the use of computers is very important. Much of the work stimulated by the appropriate use of the computer in the curriculum will take place away from the machine. It is not unreasonable to suggest that the interest children take in presenting their work in a variety of fonts and colours,

in using the bold, italic, underline and tab functions, will transfer to their handwritten efforts. Most adults are thrilled when they first produce an attractive piece of prose or poetry on the computer, and the pride and self-esteem this can generate in children should not be underestimated. Children from a school in Somerset, for example, took part in a project which provided a personal portable computer for everyone. In addition to a range of beneficial effects on IT capability, their teachers noticed renewed interest and general improvement in conventional presentation.

Communicating Information: Art

Information technology exists as an additional tool and medium within art and design. This provides real freedom for the pupil to experiment and explore through the creative and design processes, in ways that conventional art-making materials cannot always provide. However, it would be inappropriate to consider the use of computers in art and design as separate to daily classroom art activities. With pupils' entitlement to IT experience in mind, teachers will need to plan the use of computers as a part of their normal art practice. In addition, the use of computers should never be considered as a substitute to gaining the fundamental art skills through the use of conventional art media. The computer cannot provide that essential level of interaction, or the feel of real art materials. It is important therefore to identify what the computer and appropriate software can do, and utilize this as an additional contribution to the development of pupils' art, craft and design education.

As pupils begin to use the computer to explore the potential of the medium, their images may well be less sophisticated than those created using paint or pastels. However, their developing understanding and control will enable them to produce images and designs of great subtlety and variety. They will be able to explore ideas and options through choices offered by menus containing colour palettes, drawing tools, marks and textures. There are temptations to play and to move off task. But we understand the importance of play within interactive learning, and there is as much need for a teacher's involvement and direction as with any other practical activity.

This chapter examines the development of appropriate computer technology and the importance and value to the art and design curriculum that this presents. Issues of IT entitlement within art and design will be addressed, and there are examples of the ways in which appropriate technology and software can enrich and extend the primary art curriculum through projects that reflect aspects of current practice.

USING COMPUTERS WITHIN THE PRIMARY CURRICULUM

Computers have been in primary schools for many years now, and their use within some curriculum areas is well established. The developments in technology that control the power and capabilities of the computer have in many ways bypassed the primary curriculum. Much of the traditional software for the whole curriculum continues to be available, and many familiar computer systems are still working well, supported by the continued development of new software. Although the cost of the new technology has dropped in real terms, the principal issue for many primary schools has been one of inadequate funds to upgrade to more powerful computers, particularly while they have insufficient computers to meet the needs of the National Curriculum. The continued pace of change and the development of the National Curriculum has placed considerable burdens on primary teachers. The increased information on what to teach has not always been accompanied by practical help about where and how to use computers; however, the official guidance document for IT has begun to address these issues.

WHAT ARE THE CHANGES IN TECHNOLOGY THAT NOW DEFINE THE FUTURE OF ART AND DESIGN TEACHING?

Over the past ten years, we have moved from a computer that offered a limited colour range (8–16 colours), with low definition (large pixels) and limited options for the manipulation and development of the image, to computer systems that offer increased ranges of colour (256–16.7 million colours) and high-definition images; high-quality monitors (computer screens); cheaper and better colour printers; image grabbing and manipulation devices; and software that operates in a manner consistent with conventional art-making, and in a way that reinforces skills and develops art and design concepts as part of normal art practice. There is a temptation to wait for this 'white heat of technology development' to stop, before we think about coming to terms with the demands of this new technology.

DO WE REALLY NEED THESE DEVELOPMENTS?

For art and design particularly, the answer is yes, but such a judgement needs qualification. We have just reached a point in the development of the hardware where the quality of the screen image is as consistent with traditional art materials as might be expected, and indeed, often better. Computer printers in

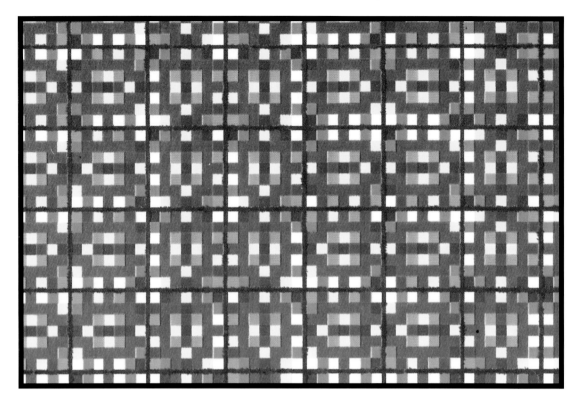

Figure 4.1 Examples of repeat patterns using 8 and 256 colours

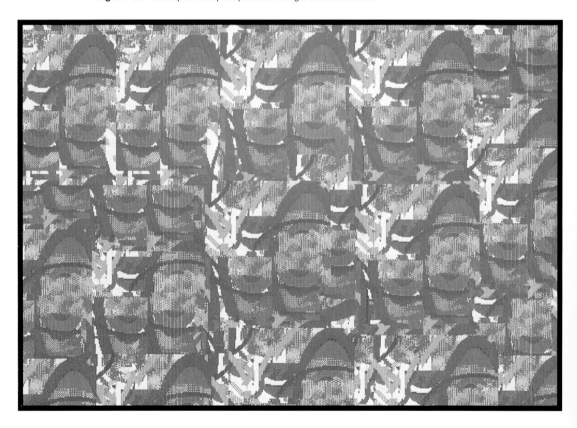

general, and particularly colour printers, are now developing to keep pace with the quality of the screen image. Software too has developed, and art and design software offers opportunities to fully explore the whole process of mark-making, line, tone, colour-mixing, shape, form and pattern work to develop concepts and understanding through exploration (Figure 4.1). Pupils can save the stages of development of their work, exploring with confidence as ideas occur to them, returning later to select and print appropriate images. There are additional peripheral devices that allow digital/video photography and drawn images to be transferred to the screen and used in a more flexible way than traditional collage and picture-building activities allow. In addition, operating systems have developed, enabling teachers with little previous knowledge of computers to explore the creative possibilities within art and design activities.

We must also be aware of the enormous contribution of the home computer to the development of IT skills, experience and understanding gained by pupils. The recent growth in this market and the fact that many parents now have computers for their own work at home, mean that some pupils often have access to more sophisticated systems than those provided at school. This in itself is creating considerable pressures in terms of motivation, when pupils are faced with using what they define as 'obsolete' technology. Their view of the development for this technology is very different from ours. They are not threatened. They are confident and see the new technologies as offering greater flexibility and providing exciting options to explore. They might make the analogy of comparing new technologies with old: drawing with chunky felt pens, as compared with having the option to select from a whole range of exciting mark-making materials. In short, they may be aware of the limitations of the old technology.

A very different function of the use of IT is beginning to be identified through the use of the CD-ROM in art and design. New titles are slowly emerging, predominantly on the PC Windows and Macintosh platforms. At present, these disks fall into three main categories:

1. Those produced by the major British and international galleries, e.g. the National and Tate Galleries;
2. Significant international collections;
3. A focus on a particular art movement.

These CD-ROM disks offer an alternative approach to the area of critical studies (Attainment Target 2 – Knowledge and understanding) by providing a valuable resource for teachers to use for discussion and investigation purposes. Containing a library of images (about 2000 images per disk) and some text, these disks are produced generally for the home market or secondary schools. However, they represent excellent value for money when compared to purchasing art books, and the text provides a useful briefing for teachers.

IN WHAT WAY IS THE COMPUTER AN APPROPRIATE TOOL TO USE WITHIN ART AND DESIGN ACTIVITIES?

We will need to ask some pertinent questions to help us identify this role and function:

- What can the computer do most effectively?
- How can we integrate IT into what we are presently doing?
- How do we structure and organize the use of IT?
- How do we ensure equal and appropriate opportunity?

What can the computer do most effectively?

The computer encourages exploration of ideas and experimentation. Pupils can: change images, try colour combinations, repeat patterns, enlarge and reduce, rotate, animate and compose on screen. Most of these activities can be achieved by pupils with various skill and ability levels, because they can continually save their work and experiment without fear of ruining or losing their designs and drawings. This process is consistent with normal good practice, but it can be hard for children with little confidence to explore and stretch their abilities with conventional art materials. This mode of working is rapid and allows pupils to test ideas as they occur. In particular, exploring the many options in repeat pattern work allows pupils to create pattern and repeats that would not be possible through conventional means and only partly through full access to a photocopier (Figure 4.2).

The very nature of much of the new software encourages investigation and opportunities for choice. Some software begins by inviting the format and size of paper to be selected. Menus are selected and placed on the screen adjacent to the paper/drawing window. The *Toolbox* menu provides recognizable icons supporting the transfer of skills and understanding. Types and sizes of mark have to be selected and can be customized. Colour can be selected or new colours and patterns mixed. Pupils willingly make all these choices and develop an understanding of the implications of their decisions. There is no preciousness. Mistakes can be easily corrected or they can return to the last saved version. There are many outcomes, not just a single drawing or painting. The process is evident in the work and this aids assessment. More importantly, the pupils have made choices, often in a way that they will not when using conventional art media. How many brush sizes and shapes will pupils usually select, and how many colours would they normally mix when using paint? This has an effect back in the classroom and they are then more likely to make these selections in future.

How can we integrate IT into what we are presently doing?

In effective art and design teaching, the computer is used as a part of the drawing and designing process. It gives pupils the freedom to experiment and explore and can be integrated into cross-curricular activities and all aspects of topic work.

paint/draw: observe, analyse, record from experience and imagination. Make marks to identify the vocabulary of the software. Explore still-life, portraits, objects, animals and landscape and respond to a stimulus. (Figure 4.3b)

collage: cut/copy and create designs by blending and adding selected images together.

illustrate: create book covers or their own books, cartoon characters, explore simple animation, sequences, work from storyboards, illustrations to accompany text or poetry. (Figure 4.3a)

pattern   textile designs, fashion, repeat prints, tiling, rotation, flip/ mirroring, wrapping paper, wallpaper and colour sets. NB explore links with mathematics. (Figure 4.3c)

colour: colour range, limited palette, colour wash, tonal palette, colour mixing and colour-ways. (Figure 4.5a, b)

graphics: packaging, designing, book covers, logo designs, 3-D and product designs, cards, posters font/text manipulation and games.

CD-ROM: explore works of art, analyse and deconstruct images. As a class or group demonstration tool or for individuals and small groups.

NB   With the addition of a colour printer the computer allows pupils to print the evidence of the process they have worked though. A sequence of stored images can be recalled and printed.

How do we structure and organize the use of IT?

- Ensure that the contexts for the use of computers within art and design are largely consistent with normal art practice; do not seek to create new contexts for IT to be used by pupils.

- Through the selection of appropriate hardware and software, we should seek to develop consistency and continuity of transferable skills.

- Use the art Programmes of Study to define the range of contexts for the use of IT.

Figure 4.2a Starting from a water colour by Sarah Bell, artist-in-residence

Figure 4.2b Digitalized image from the centre of the picture

Figure 4.2c Motifs cut from the digitalized image

Figure 4.2d Large motif: a drop repeat pattern

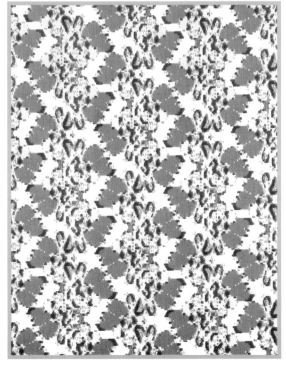

Figure 4.2e Small motif: rotated with a half drop

Figure 4.2f Several motifs mirrored and dropped

Within these general aims, structured activities may have the following specific aims:

1. explore the visual elements – awareness of colour, line, shape, tone, pattern, texture form and space;
2. provide opportunities for creative, imaginative and expressive outcomes;
3. encourage experimentation and the exploration of ideas using the computer as an electronic sketchbook;
4. use a computer to explore the design process;
5. develop an understanding of the computer as another art and design tool.

How do we ensure equal and appropriate opportunity?

There is limited guidance on the use of IT within the art and design curriculum. The National Curriculum Art Order, only states that

> Pupils should be given opportunities, where appropriate, to develop and apply their information technology (IT) capability in their study of art, craft and design.

Additional guidance is to be found in *Information Technology: The New Requirements* (SCAA/ACAC, 1995).

The following statements for what might be required within the primary art curriculum are offered as guidance; they are not a statutory requirement.
NB Much of this deals with generic IT skills gained across the curriculum and not therefore taught exclusively within art and design.

Key Stage 1

- Know that computers can be used as a tool for drawing and painting.
- Have appropriate opportunities to use a computer to draw, design or paint.
- With help, be able to save what they have produced.
- With help, be able to print what they have produced.

Key Stage 2

- Know that computers can be used as a tool for drawing, designing and painting.
- Know that computers can be used for many purposes in the art and design world.

- Have appropriate opportunities to use a computer to draw, design or paint as part of current art work.

- Be able to open a file, develop, modify and save what they have produced.

- Be able to print what they have produced.

- Be able to select a printer type (colour/black and white) to produce a printed image.

- Be able to add/combine text with an image.

- Be able to cut/copy and paste to create a new image from another image.

CHOOSING A COMPUTER

The two main types of computer in use within schools have already been described. We should now explore the advantages and disadvantages of these computers so that we can make a judgement as to their relative merits.

The first generation computers (limited colour and low definition) have adequate primary art and design software available for them. The limitation of eight to sixteen colours is not a real difficulty, although it would be helpful if there was some control over the choice of these colours. The real limitation in some of these machines is the drawing tool (pointing device).

How are the children going to make marks and draw using this computer?

These machines are not generally provided with any form of pointing device, and many children resort to the use of the cursor keys. This is slow and cumbersome and can not really be thought of as drawing. It is possible, however, to purchase a mouse, joystick, trackerball or a graphpad to come as close as possible to the physical act of drawing.

The new generation of computers developed over the last seven years are powerful and sophisticated. They are well suited to all forms of graphics and design work giving you a choice of 256 colours from a total of 4096 or up to 16.7 million colours depending on the platform, model and operating system selected. They have a sensitive mouse as a pointing device and a range of very powerful and extremely flexible and interactive software packages to support art and design activities. The mouse can be replaced with a graphics tablet, which provides an electronic pen and drawing tablet to allow greater control. A large number of add-on modules and internal upgrades are available. These facilitate video digitizing and scanning, but can be expensive to purchase.

Figure 4.3a Illustrate
Figure 4.3b Paint/Draw

Figure 4.3c (above) Pattern

Figure 4.3d (below) Exploring colour

Identifying appropriate art software

When purchasing software the following points should be considered:

- Does it meet the needs of the art curriculum and will it support other curriculum use? NB Art packages are generally used for many functions within a primary school.
- Does it offer sufficient scope for the most able?
- Is it too difficult for all pupils to use?
- Is it affordable?
- Will it last, or will it be out of date very quickly? (Is there an upgrade route?)
- Does it offer progression? (Is there continuity between the gradually more sophisticated packages used in key stages, or is it one of a common set of art packages used with both primary and secondary schools?)

Some useful rules for selection are:

- Buy only what you will use. Unused hardware and software is a waste.
- Choose software that:
  – will give pupils opportunities to explore and manipulate images;
  – will not restrict pupils' creativity;
  – is flexible;
  – will last;
  – will operate and develop skills consistent with normal art practice;
  – provides good support, i.e. handbook/manual, etc.

We often underestimate the abilities of pupils particularly with respect to computers. We must offer them the opportunities to use appropriate software within the context of realistic tasks.

Peripheral devices

It is possible to obtain a number of peripheral devices to plug into your computer. They extend the range of activities that are possible. The following allow you to input/output digital information or images in a variety of ways:

- *Electronic photography*. A digitizer is a device that converts a video signal from a video camera, video still cameras or VCR to a picture on the computer screen. This can then be manipulated and used within many software art packages. (Figure 4.5)

- ***Electronic photocopy.*** A scanner is a small hand-held device (A4/A5) or flatbed (A4) that allows photographs, drawings, text and images of all kinds to be transferred to the screen and then used, as above. Colour versions are available.

- ***Drawing device***. A graphpad or graphics tablet can replace the mouse as a pointing device. This is a more accurate form of control, allowing tracing of an image, but is expensive.

- ***CD-ROM player***. Like a CD player in a hi-fi system, but more flexible. It will play images, text, sound and film images, all controlled by the computer it is connected to.

- ***Pointing devices***. Other forms of pointing device include the touch pad, touch screen, joystick and trackerball. These facilitate ease of control, particularly in the case of some pupils with particular individual needs.

Although peripheral devices are expensive, it is worth considering shared ownership between schools, for example as part of a cluster or consortium.

Printing

There are three main printer types in schools: ink jet, dot matrix and laser. They come in various forms and vary enormously in price. Always ask for printed samples before purchasing a printer. Better still, keep an image you know well, on disk and obtain a print for comparison from each of the printers you are considering. Consider and compare the following issues:

- cost per print;
- cost of replacement ink cartridges/toner;
- specialist paper or available as standard (plain paper?);
- lifespan of the printer (number of printed sheets);
- speed to print an image or page of text;
- size of printer and size of printout;
- ease of use and maintenance needs.

Ink jet printers

It must be understood that the output of any printer will differ from the original screen image. Colour printers create their image through four inks being combined in a subtractive manner onto the paper. Computer monitor screens produce a colour image by mixing the emitted light from three dots in an additive manner. It is important therefore to understand the limitations of the

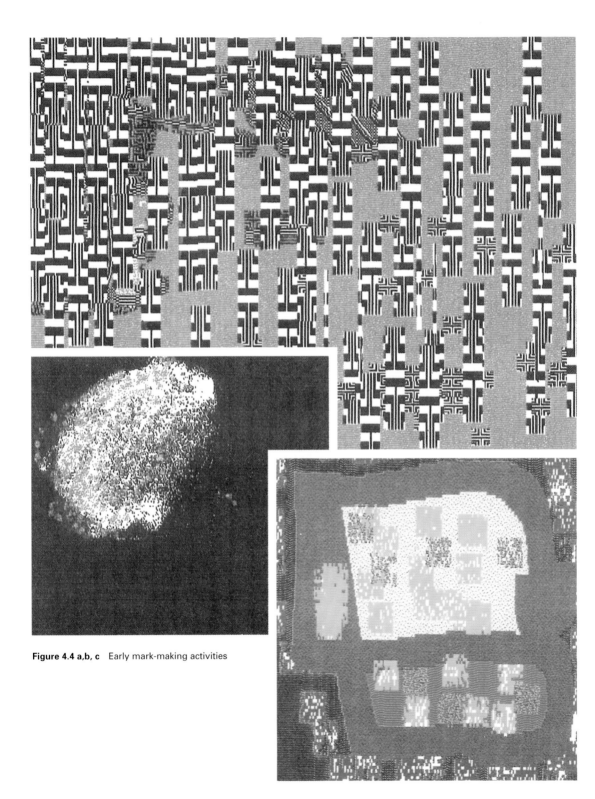

Figure 4.4 a,b, c Early mark-making activities

Figure 4.5a Wrought iron chair pattern

Figure 4.5b Re-coloured from digitalized image

printing process with present technology. However, this only means that not all printers are capable of the subtle colour ranges that the computer screen can display. This limitation should not restrict the activities of pupils, and only really has an effect when pupils wish to reproduce exactly what they have on screen.

Paper. It is important to use the proper coated paper, for ink jet printers, as plain or non-specialist papers can produce very poor results. Acetate is also available, but is generally very expensive and takes considerable time to dry. NB You can use some forms of handmade textured paper in many ink jet printers. Fabriano works very well and generally gives good colour rendition.

Fabric. Some companies produce Sublimatic inks that allow you to transfer a print to fabric using a hot iron. NB It is not recommended that you try to put fabric directly through an ink jet printer.

Dot matrix printers

Dot matrix printers are used mainly as a way of printing text. They operate like a typewriter with pins that strike the page through a black ribbon. This allows you to print in black and white, use coloured paper, or produce a limited range of grey tones on white paper. There are printers of this type that produce colour using a coloured ribbon set. However, they are a not particularly effective and costly alternative to ink jet printers. NB Interesting effects can be achieved by printing onto metallic foil, metallic backed paper or acetate.

Laser printers

Produced mainly as black-and-white printers, but now also grey tone ranges and colour. These machines are rather like a photocopier, producing high-definition images. They are most suitable for printing text and desktop publishing pages (combined text and images), particularly when these prints are to be reprinted for distribution or publishing. High-contrast images can print effectively and various half-tone options are available.

WORKING WITH A WHOLE CLASS

There are still not large numbers of computers in the primary classroom. Some schools have created computer rooms or clusters with a small number of machines. However, access to a single machine should not restrict drawing, designing or experimental activities occurring within the classroom. It will of course be necessary to find a means of ensuring that all pupils have these opportunities to use a computer. This may be achieved through individual, paired or small-group work, or a rota system. The teacher might also use one machine as a demonstration machine or teaching aid (perhaps to explain a concept, demonstrate a process or show images from a CD-ROM). Although some pupils may wish to use the computer for many activities, others may not wish to use it at all. However, all pupils have an entitlement to experience and to use IT.

The way in which the whole school uses its computers should be considered. For example, should they be on trolleys and flexible enough to be moved between classrooms at times, to create temporary clusters for particular projects?

EXPLORING PROJECTS

All of these projects have been devised to address issues of IT capability and fully comply with the requirements of the National Curriculum Order for Art. This is not a definitive list and these are not complete projects, just starting-points for exploring how a computer can contribute to the creative process.

Mark-making and visual vocabulary exercises

Aim

To develop an understanding of the potential of the computer as an art medium.

Project outline

Explore the visual elements of line, tone, colour, pattern, shape and space, through mark-making exercises. This will enable pupils to develop an understanding of the vocabulary of the software. They can explore draw and paint options such as the quality of line that computers can produce, mark widths, colour mixing, drawing with pattern and shapes (Figure 4.4).

This exercise will act as an introduction to the computer and should be seen as a parallel activity to conventional mark-making investigations with unfamiliar art media. Pupils should save their completed screens and print out pages to stick into their sketchbooks. They might extend this activity by exploring conventional art materials in the same way and comparing the results. These activities would then lead into a structured art project on the computer.

Self portraits

Aim

To develop an understanding of how the computer can be used as a drawing tool to work from observation or experience.

Figure 4.6a–d A sequence of images taken from a video film, digitalized and true colour saturation altered

Figure 4.6a–d (cont'd)

Project outline

Through the draw and paint options, pupils can use the computer as a drawing and painting tool to build up a portrait head picture. A mirror can be attached to the computer monitor to help a pupil produce a self-portrait, or they can work from memory. Collect examples of faces in books and magazines, or look at artists' portraits to help prepare pupils.

This exercise allows pupils to explore the outline and proportions of a portrait, making changes and overpainting before placing features such as eyes, nose and ears. If features are drawn in the wrong place or at the wrong scale, they can be altered. Pupils can explore building up layers of colour for hair with transparent washes. This supports the less able or those with little confidence.

Electronic photography

Aim

To develop an understanding of how the computer can be used to capture video images as digital photographs.

Project outline

Using a video or video still camera, record some film or take photographs in the grounds of the school, in your classroom, or of an event or a person. Play this image back and load it into the computer. When in the computer, try altering the colour balance, moving the features around on a face using copy and paste (computer Frankenstein), try stretching or distorting parts of an image, adding something into a picture, mixing different images together.

Your computer will need to be fitted with a digitizer, to perform the image capture function. Digitizers are available in monochrome and colour outputs. They are installed either directly into the computer or in a separate box. The video camera, video recorder or video still camera will need to be connected directly to the computer with the correct lead. Through the use of the digitizer software, the image can be transferred directly to the screen. Most digitizers have software that allows some manipulation of the image and certainly the colour balance. Once captured on screen, the image can be saved as a file or directly into an art package where it can be explored using all of the art package options (Figure 4.6).

Scanning from a sketchbook

Aim

To transfer drawn images into the computer to enable further exploration and experimentation

Project outline

Scanners are like digitizers. They transfer an image into digital information. Small hand-held models are connected by a cable to the computer and will normally allow you to capture an image from about the size of a postcard up to A4. They copy an image as you slowly pull them across the surface of the image. Once transferred to the computer screen, you are able to save as a file and explore the image within an art package. Try adding colour, spray or wash to a line drawing scanned from a sketchbook (Figure 4.6).

Combining images and text

Aim

To explore how images and text can be created and then combined on screen.

Project outline

This will allow you to explore poetry and accompanying images, illustrated short stories, cartoon images, posters and storyboards. Collect examples of these forms of images and text and use them to present this concept. Demonstrate and explore how the computer can create different letter styles (fonts) and alter the style and size of each letter, word or block of text. Pupils can either produce and place text on or around an image or paint an image adjacent to the text.

Repeat patterns

Aim

To explore how repeat patterns can be produced using any or all of the following options: cut/copy and paste, rotate, scale, mirror/flip. NB Some software has a motif or pattern option that will allow repeat patterns to be explored within a simple screen window.

Project outline

Collect examples of repeat patterns on paper and fabric. Discuss how the pattern repeats: does it tile or mirror, or does each part of the pattern repeat in a shifted position up or down in relation to the first image? You might want to link this work to mathematics and explore the common principles. Pupils can produce a small piece of drawing on the screen and, using copy and paste, explore the repeat options. Save screens as they are produced and print out and compare the patterns.

Logo design

Aim
To explore how letters or text can be combined with simple shapes.

Project outline
Collect and discuss examples of logos, and explore how text and simple shapes can be combined to produce a logo that will communicate clearly. Pupils can use either their own initials or the name of someone for their lettering. They will need to explore how text can be created and manipulated on screen, e.g. text size, type, style, rotation, cut/copy and paste. Try using simple geometric shapes, e.g. circles, squares, triangles and polygons to work with your letters. Explore the positioning of all letters and shapes together. Test out designs by producing different versions of your logo and discussing them.

Book cover design

Aim
To explore how text and images can be combined to communicate effectively.

Project outline
Collect and discuss examples of book covers. Produce an outline on screen of the correct size for your book. You can also use software that will allow you to open a screen of exactly the correct size. Pupils can draw or paint images into the outline or screen and then create and place the title and author. Remember that you can often rotate text or assemble letters individually for particular effects. This works effectively for pupils' own books and when linked with English or creative writing projects. Most printers will print to the screen size and, using glue and card, you can make up your book cover.

Stamp design

Aim
To produce personalized stamps and understand that the scale of images can be changed when printing.

Project outline
Collect and discuss examples of stamps. The teacher can make portrait and landscape format stamp shapes as files. These can be saved and opened by pupils when they begin their work. These stamp shapes should have a scalloped edge to simulate the perforated stamp edges. Pupils can then paint their own pictures into the empty stamp files and add a value and even a queen's head! When printing, experiment with reducing the scale until you can produce the most detailed print possible with your printer.

Communicating Information: Music

INTRODUCTION

'Let's listen to the tree again.' 'How about a mug then two apples?'

This will be familiar language if you have used the computer program *Compose*, where pictures on the computer screen represent short musical phrases which pupils arrange to form a composition. Whether or not you have used music software before, this chapter aims to explore how IT, particularly music software, can be used to support learning in music.

The music National Curriculum requires that:

Pupils should be given opportunities, where appropriate, to develop their information technology (IT) capability in their study of music [and] . . . should be taught to generate and communicate their ideas in different forms using . . . sound. (Key Stages 1 and 2 of the National Curriculum, January 1995.)

What should I be doing musically?

Perhaps before looking at some examples of music software in use, we should look broadly at the aims of music education. Music should give opportunities for pupils to engage in musical activities: composing, performing, and listening and appraising. At the same time pupils should be developing their understanding of musical elements such as pitch, rhythm, speed, dynamics or structure. Few music programs aim to cover all the activities and elements at the same time. Some deliberately concentrate on particular elements, for instance rhythm programs that focus on pupils creating, refining and sequencing rhythm patterns. Other programs concentrate on only one musical activity, such as software that develops listening skills through correctly sequencing sections of a well-known tune to recreate the original. As teachers, we need to be aware of what the software we are using is intended to develop, so that we can see how it contributes to the pupils' overall understanding in the subject.

How can I develop IT capability?

Most music software falls within the communicating and handling information theme as it develops children's ability to create and express ideas. Some software can also be said to develop the second theme. For example, where pupils try out how a musical composition would sound with different sampled instrument combinations to simulate having a number of real instrumentalists to hand, they are modelling; where music software is controlling the sounds of a MIDI keyboard, aspects of measurement and control are being developed; where pupils discuss the differences between composing a tune at the computer and using conventional classroom instruments, they may investigate parallels with the use of IT in the wider world.

What sorts of software are available?

Like the software for many subjects, music software can be grouped into two main categories: programs that are essentially closed, in that they test the pupils on things they may or may not know, perhaps including some basic instruction; and programs that offer a broader environment with less direction, but in which pupils can work more freely with a wide range of possible outcomes. Software, for instance, that tests pupils' abilities to recognize crotchets and quavers and gives them a score at the end falls into the first category. Software that offers the musical equivalent of a word processor falls into the second. In general, the latter is to be recommended as it offers the best learning outcomes and a greater flexibility for a wider range of pupils. Open-ended programs frequently represent better value for money, as less software is generally needed.

CLASSROOM SNAPSHOTS

To help us understand the use of some pieces of music software, there follow three snapshots of classroom use. It should be emphasized that the programs mentioned are suitable for use at a range of ages depending on the context of the work and the previous experience of the children.

Using *Compose World* with Year 1/2

In the first class, mixed Year 1 and 2 pupils are having an introduction to a program that allows short musical phrases, represented by pictures, to be listened to and then sequenced together to form longer sections (*Compose/Compose World*). The pupils are sitting on the carpet where they can all see the screen of the computer. The teacher is introducing the program by playing a few of the phrases and encouraging the pupils to sing them. As well as helping them to remember the fragments of melody, this is developing their sense of pitch. The teacher moves her hand in the air to show the way the pitch of the phrase moves. Some of the pupils imitate her. She asks them questions about the phrases. Which one do you think will make a good beginning to our tune? Which one do you think will fit next? Which one will make a good ending? Why? She emphasizes that there is no 'right' answer – merely a number of possibilities, some of which will sound better than others to most people. The pupils collectively 'compose' a tune by sequencing together eight phrases.

Having introduced the program in this way and shown the pupils how to save their own work, the pupils work in pairs at the computer to compose their own eight-phrase tune. The teacher has prepared a simple help card to sit beside the computer that reminds the pupils of the basic key-presses.

Each group saves their work. Some more able pupils find out how to change the speed of the piece and experiment with this.

At the end of the week, the tunes are loaded back in one at a time and performed to the rest of the class. The teacher encourages the pupils to comment on what they hear. Do they all sound the same? Has everybody chosen to end with the same phrase? Which picture have the different groups started and ended on? Has anybody used particular patterns or repetition?

The work on the computer was only part of what the teacher had planned. The overall theme for the term was 'Stories' and the pupils were writing stories based on a series of events. In their music lessons they were working with classroom instruments and their voices to compose pieces of music based on simple sequences of events represented pictorially on cards.

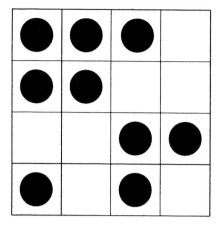 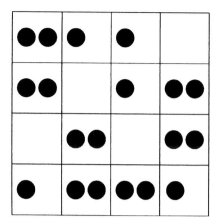

Figure 5.1   Rhythm squares

How was this activity contributing to the pupils' musical understanding, and in what way was their IT capability being developed? Musically the pupils were learning to listen carefully, to select and sequence sounds, and to store sound on a disk for later performance. They were also learning that their own choices in compositions may be different from those of others. In relation to IT, the program is clearly focused on the communication and handling of information. Pupils were learning to manipulate information in the form of sound and to store and retrieve information.

Using the computer in this way allowed the pupils to concentrate more on the activities of composing and listening, while reducing the need for them to be able to perform what they were composing.

Using *Notate* with Year 3/4

In another class, as part of work on rhythm, Year 3 and 4 pupils have been learning about one-beat notes, rests and half-beat notes through the use of simple rhythm squares where each box represents one beat of the pulse. Each box has simple blobs to represent individual notes. (Figure 5.1)

Some pupils have been helped by the use of words for the different types of beat, e.g. one-beat note – 'fly', two half-beat notes – 'spi-der', one-beat rest – 'moth'. They then moved on to composing and performing their own rhythm squares on paper.

The teacher ensures that pupils have understood the basic idea of sounds being represented by symbols. This done, the pupils are ready for the introduction of a music program that uses traditional music notation (*Notate*).

With the class sitting so that they can all see the computer, the teacher introduces one-beat notes, half-beat notes and rests, showing how they are represented on screen, stressing the similarity with the rhythm square work they are already familiar with. They are working at a very simple level, using just rhythms, with no pitch to worry about.

Together the class works out a four-bar rhythm pattern. The teacher shows how the first bar can be copied to make bars 2 and 3 by using the copy facility. She shows how changes to the notes in a bar of music can be made easily so that ideas can be created, listened to, selected, modified or rejected. The pupils are also shown how the sound for the pattern can be altered by selecting from a wide range of sampled instruments.

In groups the pupils are now set the task of composing an eight-bar pattern. Some use repetition and contrast as part of their pattern using cut and paste. They select suitable instruments for their pattern from the stock of sampled sounds. Some groups work in two parts by composing a second pattern to fit with their first pattern. One particularly able pair even manage to compose in four parts, each with a different instrumental sound. This group later go on to compose a sixteen-bar pattern in four parts, each with a different instrumental sound. Part of this was done during a lunchtime break.

All groups save their compositions on disk and print them out to perform them on conventional classroom instruments. Later the pupils talk about the difference between composing rhythm patterns on the computer and working on paper.

As part of their work the class listened to and talked about other music that featured strong rhythm patterns including marches and West African drumming.

Again, what musical ideas were being developed and what aspects of IT capability? The pupils' understanding of rhythms and rhythm notation was obviously being developed. In addition their understanding of the appropriate use of instruments for performing rhythm patterns was enhanced. Although the pupils were principally involved in the activity of composing while at the computer, the remainder of the work was planned to maintain a reasonable balance of musical activities. In relation to IT, pupils worked within the communicating information strand when creating, modifying and refining their ideas. Having composed rhythm patterns on paper and at the computer, the pupils were in a good position to develop their understanding of the applications and effects of IT.

Using *Notate* with Year 5/6 pupils

In a Year 5/6 class, pupils are already used to singing rounds in a number of parts and are now being encouraged to think about composing their own. First

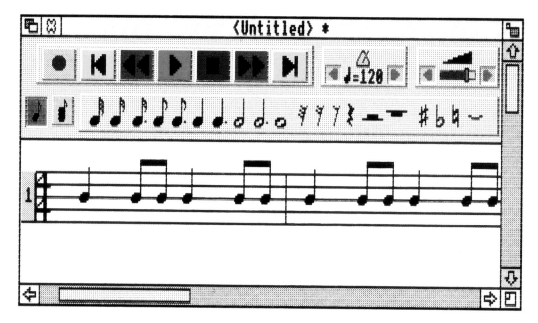

Figure 5.2 Rhythm track using *Notate*

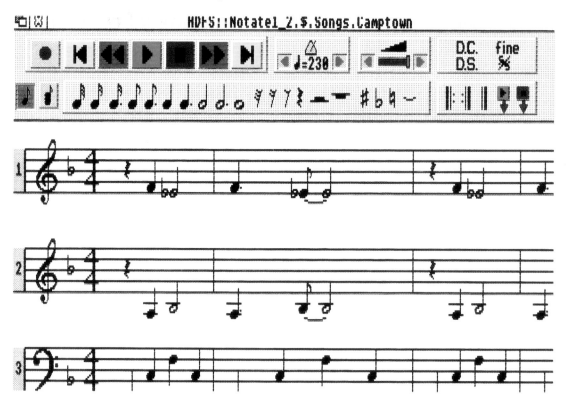

Figure 5.3 'Here's one I composed earlier!'

Figure 5.4   'That should be a crotchet!'

they use their voices and melodic instruments to explore how groups of notes sound when played together. Next they explore the written form of these chords using notation. They then investigate why a round they know 'works', recognizing the chords that are used.

Finally, using an electronic music keyboard linked to the computer via MIDI (Musical Instrument Digital Interface) and the computer program *Notate*, pupils work in groups to create their own rounds (Figures 5.2, 5.3). The teacher suggests that pupils use the note C to start and end.

The computer program is used to realize the rounds and provide immediate confirmation of the success or otherwise of the results. Groups are able to change notes and replay their rounds until they are satisfied. The cut and paste facility makes it quick to copy the first part to make the second entry of the round. The computer being linked to the electronic music keyboard enables pupils to play their rounds on a variety of quality instrument and synthesizer sounds. All groups manage to complete the task, save and print their work.

Musically, the pupils were developing their listening skills, their understanding of pitch, notation and the structure of rounds. Their IT capability was being developed through creating, amending and presenting within the medium of sound. The pupils were also learning that the computer could control an external device (an electronic music keyboard).

MIDI (Musical Instrument Digital Interface) is a system whereby computers, keyboards and other equipment can exchange musical information. For instance a keyboard might be connected to a computer so that the tunes being played from the computer would sound on the keyboard. A keyboard might also be connected to a computer so that notes played on the keys would end up as notation on the computer screen.

The computer here is not used as the central focus of the activity. Instead it is merely a tool used at an appropriate point within an activity to enable the learning objectives to be more easily achieved. Without the computer program, it would be necessary to have proficient singers or instrumentalists to discover whether the rounds 'worked'. However, by working on the computer each group was able, within an afternoon, to hear if their rounds worked, and if not, to analyse why.

Summary of classroom snapshots

In the examples above, what are the characteristics of the use of IT to develop understanding in music?

- The software was used to help develop pupils' understanding of musical concepts. The learning in both music and IT was planned and relevant.

- IT was not seen as an alternative to conventional musical activities.

- Pupils were given a specific task as part of a progression of activities, rather than being allowed to wander aimlessly.

- Pupils were able to respond at a variety of levels depending on their previous experience – the software allowed the tasks to be differentiated by outcome.

- Teachers were familiar with the software they were using.

- The work at the computer was linked with practical use of classroom percussion instruments.

- Time was set aside for performance and discussion.

- There was a balance of whole-class and group use of the computer as appropriate for the task.

- Work was saved, even when it was very short.

LISTENING AND APPRAISING

The programs mentioned above are not the only ones available. Many programs exist across a range of computers that offer exciting possibilities for teachers. As well as programs similar to those mentioned above, there are other avenues being opened up to music through new technology. Perhaps one of the most promising is CD-ROM. With this it is possible for pupils to have access to lengthy recordings of sounds and music, some of them with video stills or clips. The possibilities of CD-ROM to support aspects of listening and appraising within music are enormous.

PLANNING

As with any subject, the use of software to enhance learning in music needs to be planned. This means careful overall whole-school planning to get the position of each program in a suitable stage within the school. It's no good the Year 5/6 teachers starting work with *Compose*, only to realize the children have all 'done it before Miss!' In teachers' own planning it means making appropriate links with the rest of their work in music, in IT and in the other subjects of the curriculum. It also means looking at the entitlement of all pupils to work with suitable software at an appropriate level for them.

Some teachers plan so that everybody has an opportunity to work through a basic sequence of activities at their own level. At a later stage, there are further opportunities for some pupils to work at a higher level or follow a particular interest. In some schools this may be as part of an extra-curricular activity.

Music software need not take up an enormous amount of time, although it easily could. Basically, pupils need sufficient time at the computer to carry out the activity successfully. This does not mean all day every day though! The quality of the time pupils are at the computer is in the end more important than the quantity.

CONCLUSIONS

Teachers start to make use of music software for different reasons: some established music teachers like the ease with which music can be written out using traditional notation for recorder groups, orchestras, etc.; those who feel uneasy about teaching music may see music software as an avenue into music-making.

Whichever category you fall into, music software can enhance teaching in a number of ways, through:

- enabling pupils who may have no particular performance skill to create music;

- enabling individuals or groups to play more complex music then they would otherwise be able to;

- allowing pupils to experiment with the 'what if' type of environment and know that they can alter what they create, in the same way as with a word processor;

- allowing pupils to concentrate on the activities of composing and listening while lessening the importance of high-level performance skills.

IT opens up enormous and exciting possibilities within music. Although many pupils in key stages 1 and 2 will only be using music software at a relatively simple level, the seeds are being sown for the future – seeds that for some will grow into something tremendously important in their later schooling or beyond.

The use of some music software can alter the balance of the importance of the different musical activities. As long as the benefits and possible disadvantages of this are recognized it can allow pupils to make progress in music in new and exciting ways.

However, perhaps one of the most important skills for the teacher is knowing when to switch the computer off and get the instruments out!

Handling Information

Information technology is all around us. Whenever there is a large amount of information to store or manipulate, IT systems offer both high storage capacity and speed of access. At any visit to a supermarket the check-out demonstrates most efficient reading of the product via a laser barcode reader and subsequent identification and cost, all within the twinkling of an eye. Our pupils are surrounded by examples of IT handling information at breathtaking speeds and efficiency. New technologies now allow full-length feature films to be stored onto a single CD-ROM, and in the near future ten, a hundred times as much information will be stored onto just such a storage medium.

The programme of study in the new orders state that at Key Stage 1, pupils should be taught to enter and store information; retrieve, process and display information that has been stored. We have to offer our pupils opportunities to develop the necessary skills to store, access and display information efficiently. Skills such as scanning, browsing, setting up logical searches and simply identifying what they are searching for are all of increasing importance, especially as more and more information can be stored within a smaller space.

At Key Stage 2 the Programme of Study states that pupils should be taught to: use IT equipment and software to organize, reorganize and analyse ideas and information; select suitable information and media, and classify and prepare information for processing with IT, checking for accuracy; interpret, analyse and check the plausibility of information held on IT systems and select the elements required for particular purposes, considering the consequences of any errors.

As pupils develop greater skills in curriculum areas such as Science AT1, they need to use IT as a tool to seek out patterns within experimental findings, check for accuracy and perhaps prove or disprove a hypothesis. By collecting the necessary data and then using appropriate software, they are not only widening their understanding and skills in that particular curriculum area but also developing their IT capability.

Information handling covers a wide range of activities: sorting, grouping, categorizing, searching and the seeking and illustration of patterns within information or data. Such activities are not new. Our pupils have been involved often within a mathematics or science context or where use of logic blocks has helped them to develop logical thinking and the appreciation of attributes.

The progression in information-handling skills is not straightforward; the existence of a hierarchy of information-handling skills is debatable. Certainly there are some fundamental concepts that have to be in place for particular development. Many such concepts should be developed away from the computer and down on the floor or on the table top as Key Stage 1 activities.

This whole area of understanding and development of skills should start with the very young and initially may have nothing to do with IT. In the early years, how do we go about offering our pupils such experiences? A rewarding exercise is to place two similar objects, like a pencil and a paintbrush, in front of a group of pupils and ask them to list six similarities and six differences that they find. If practical, most senses should be used – touch, smell, hearing and sight. As an exercise to help develop observational skills it is both practical and fun.

Many information-handling skills and concepts are based upon a firm experience base consisting of the manipulation of concrete objects, seeking similarities and differences, sorting into sets and subsets, the assigning of attributes to members of sets or whole sets and the understanding of membership of sets. Using collections of items in the classroom is a good start, and such a group of concrete objects may offer many opportunities for the development of early information-handling skills.

Pupils from class 3L were asked to bring along two kitchen utensils as part of their project on 'Our Homes'. Some of the utensils brought were wooden, some plastic and some metal. Indeed some were part-wood and part-metal and some part-plastic and part-metal. There were the usual types that cut, shredded, grated, opened, spooned, stirred, pushed, pulled, scooped, crushed and measured. The collection was a paradise of language, definitions and actions. On the floor, groups from class 3L sorted all forty items into different groups. The most obvious groupings were of materials. There was the wooden, the metal and the plastic group. Where to put the part-wooden, part-metal utensils? The appreciation of attributes is paramount in the development of information-handling skills, and these in turn are based upon observational skills and the ability to see and articulate similarities and differences.

From such a floor activity can come the understanding of subsets, the intersection of sets and the null or empty set. Similarly the use of key words to define group membership may emerge from similar activities. Key words are a useful tool in the accessing of information, but it is important that their function is fully understood.

Projects where information is readily available and clearly understood, such as homes, pets, traffic, favourite food and favourite TV programmes, are an excellent starting-point for Key Stage 1 pupils. Often such activities lead to the production of a graph or pictogram demonstrating to the pupils that particular data may be represented in pictorial form. Such graphs tell much at a glance,

Figure 6.1 'So how many are 145 centimetres?'

Figure 6.2 'Will it stay like this?'

and pupils need the experience of interpreting lists of numbers and then seeing how these numbers, when in graphical form, are easier to interpret.

Data can be listed in various ways such as in alphabetical order or in numerical order. Whether the pupils have knowledge of their alphabet or understand the ordination of numbers is critical; involvement in such an activity may well help develop these concepts anyway. The reasons for sorting data need to be explained. As an everyday example the dictionary or telephone directory is sorted in alphabetical order for one reason only – ease of access.

This simple beginning with tally chart software that offers opportunities to store, sort and plot data allows pupils to develop a firm base of understanding which will be built upon when they start to use a more sophisticated database.

Here is an account from the teacher of a Year 3 primary class:

As part of the work within the topic of 'Myself' the children had to collect certain measurements of their bodies, using various measuring devices such as measuring tapes, metre sticks and weighing scales. The children needed to be reminded of the need for accuracy and had to select the most appropriate piece of equipment for the measuring task they were involved in. They collected their data and recorded it in a variety of ways. It was decided, after discussion, that it would be a good idea if the results could be produced on a standard sheet. They were beginning to understand the need for some sort of standardised data

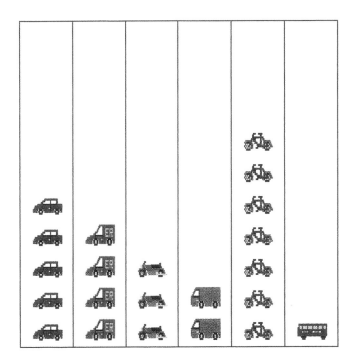

Figure 6.3 Traffic passing the school gate

collection sheet. The one they produced was used by everyone in the class (Figure 6.6).

When deciding how to design their datasheet, the children took account of the units of measurement they were going to use so that they had standard, compatible data.

It was interesting to note also, that the children were very accurate in their measuring – and also checking with each other, in a co-operative way, that they were measuring correctly, so that they didn't invalidate the survey. It was a good way of letting children see that incorrect data could affect their final results.

Once all the measuring had been completed, the children had to decide how they would store their information. It was suggested that the sheets could be stored in a file but this was thought to be old-fashioned by the children. They stated that it could be very difficult to retrieve the information, if it were to be stored in this way and it would take a long time to interrogate the information if they were looking for more than one thing at a time. The children decided that they would like to find out things about the class as a whole and set about the task of deciding how the information could be collected. They decided that, working in two's, each pair could be responsible for collating the information about one of the areas of measurement, i.e. one pair would collate leg measurement, one cubic size and so on. The children then decided that they would need to produce a datasheet so that the information could be tallied.

They obtained a class list so that they could ensure that no-one was missed out and set about collecting data from every class member. This took a long time but I felt it to be a worthwhile exercise because this led to a discussion on the best ways of storing information. The children found it difficult to collect all the information from all the children. We then looked at possible solutions to this problem and decided that it may have been quicker to produce the recording sheet as a database master and input the information straight into the computer.

It was agreed by the children that this is what we would do on future occasions. This time, however, they wanted to ascertain if their original system would work. After having some difficulty collating their data, they used the dataplot package to produce a graph of their choice, showing the results in a variety of ways. They decided that it was easier to interpret the results with the block graph and piechart.

We also looked at the 'mean' and the 'range' of the data we had collected, finding out how to calculate them. This helped when we wanted to look at average measurements of the people in the class. This work was very interesting as an introduction to the world of databases. The children soon learned that it would have been useful to have stored their initial work on a computer database so that they were able to manipulate that data much more easily and that they could then have interrogated it with a great deal more speed. A useful lesson to learn!

It was, however, an extremely useful program to use, both as an introduction to the idea of a computer database and as an introduction to the capabilities of the Archimedes computer. The children appreciated the speed of the program in utilising the capabilities of the computer, especially in the production of graphs, and this also acted as a stimulus for the children to try and produce their own.

The definition of a database is far from rigid and indeed the orders for IT do not use the word. A generic definition might be '*an organized system for the storage and access of information*'. The card index system in most school offices is a good example of a 'conventional' database. Across the key stages pupils should be offered software that increases opportunity to develop more sophisticated information-handling skills. For example, the necessity to carry out searches could be introduced at Key Stage 1. A simple search could be 'Who has most … ?' or 'On which day did it not rain?' The introduction of what is known as the logical AND/OR search, is further down the path of conceptual understanding. Most probably this kind of search would be introduced during Key Stage 2. Such a search within a database on British birds could isolate all those birds that eat insects AND lay more than six eggs. The earlier table-top sorting and setting activities should help clarify the difference between AND and OR.

Further comments from a Key Stage 2 teacher:

As part of the work in this topic, the children were going to study the weather. Each day the children collected certain information about the day's weather, using a variety of measuring instruments from the school's weather station and showed their results on a datasheet. In that way we could see at a glance what the weather was like on a particular day. It would be difficult, however, to cross reference these pieces of information without very careful observation.

Obviously, this was a good way to introduce the idea of a database using the computer, and how to use it to interrogate the data which we had collected. I selected Grass, *produced by Newman College, which, although fairly easy to use, is also a powerful database which allows very detailed records to be kept, for example up to 18 separate pieces of information on each record. There are a variety of ways of sorting the information contained, plus the ability to interrogate the data held and the construction of graphs from that information.*

The children and I soon constructed a new file to contain our weather data, using the Grass *editor facility.*

Each day the children collected the data using the weather station we had set up on their datasheets and then entered the information into the database file we had created. The children soon realised that the information had to be presented in a standard way at the same time each day. We used the database we had created to produce a weekly record of the weather, which we displayed

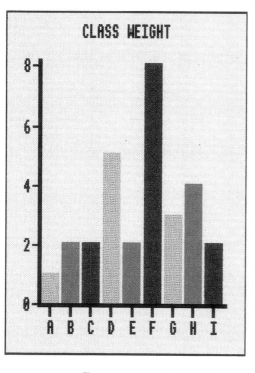

Figure 6.4 Illustrating the data

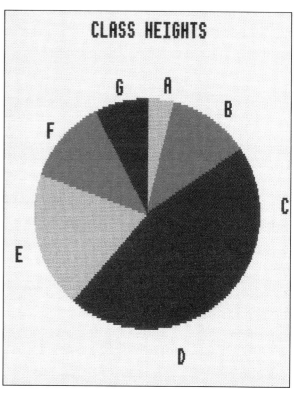

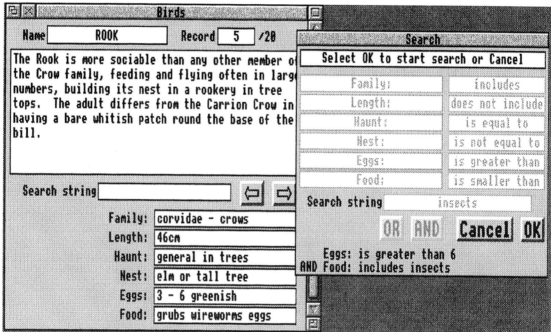

Figure 6.5 Setting the 'AND' search

we had created to produce a weekly record of the weather, which we displayed for other children, teachers and parents to look at. This created a lot of interest in the school. We were also able to look at specific parts of the record and show the results graphically.

I then asked the children to think of questions they would like to ask, with some very interesting replies! We interrogated the database in a variety of ways, even to the extent of finding out which member of staff was most likely to get wet during playground duty and which day was the best to do outdoor games! On a more serious note, it was interesting to observe that the temperature was often higher on the days it rained and the wind direction often influenced the type of weather we could expect.

Certain information-handling software allows pupils to design their own questionnaire and then use the same software to analyse the information collected (Figure 6.6). This approach is most useful for opinion survey activities.

I wanted a program that enabled the children to construct their own datasheets which could then be held on a database and manipulated in a variety of different ways. Junior Pinpoint *(by Longman Logotron), is such a program. It is*

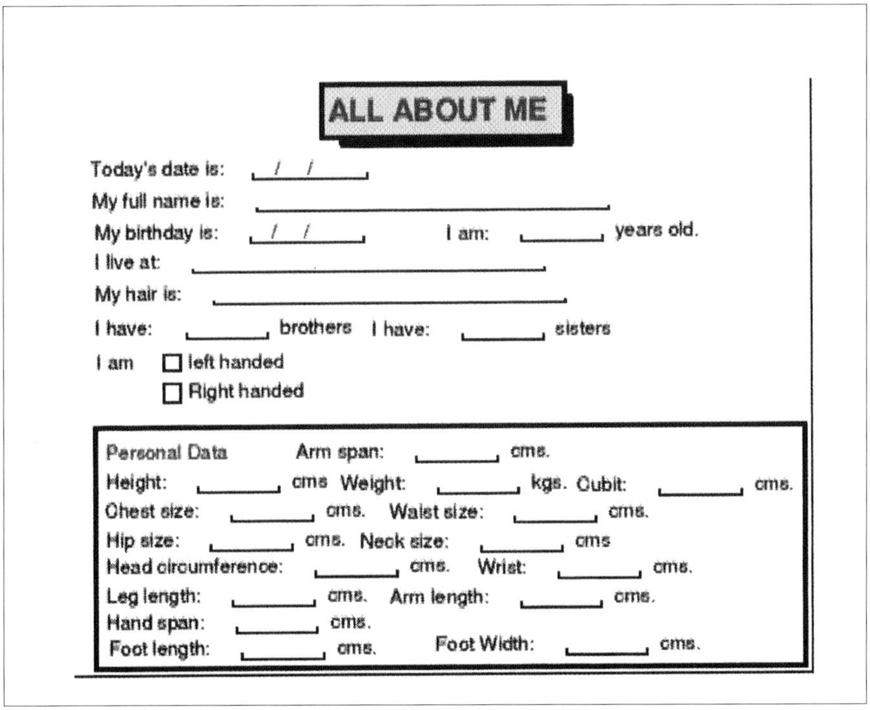

ALL ABOUT ME

Today's date is: ___/___/___
My full name is: _____
My birthday is: ___/___/___   I am: _____ years old.
I live at: _____
My hair is: _____
I have: _____ brothers   I have: _____ sisters
I am   ☐ left handed
       ☐ Right handed

Personal Data   Arm span: _____ cms.
Height: _____ cms Weight: _____ kgs. Cubit: _____ cms.
Chest size: _____ cms. Waist size: _____ cms.
Hip size: _____ cms. Neck size: _____ cms
Head circumference: _____ cms. Wrist: _____ cms.
Leg length: _____ cms. Arm length: _____ cms.
Hand span: _____ cms.
Foot length: _____ cms.   Foot Width: _____ cms.

Figure 6.6   Designing the questionnaire

questionnaires. When this has been done the information can be collected in one of two ways: it can either be entered directly into the computer or the questionnaire can be printed and photocopied and then entered into the computer.

When the database is finished it can be sorted and searched by way of a spreadsheet and results can be shown graphically. A desktop publishing package included in the program then allows the children to produce finished reports, adding lines, text and graphics to enhance their work. I decided, as part of our topic work on 'Communication', to allow the children to conduct a survey of their own choice. The children had to think of questions they would like to ask on a topic of their own choice. One child decided to look at the issue of favourite types of food and designed a questionnaire to help survey people's thoughts. Before we did this we ran through a questionnaire constructed by the class to get used to how the program worked. This was an interesting and very positive exercise which helped considerably when the children came to construct their own. We chose the same survey that we had conducted previously as part of the 'Myself' topic called 'All about me'. We chose this for two reasons. Firstly, we were familiar with the questions asked, and secondly, it gave the children the opportunity to see how much they had grown. So, using the editor page, we constructed a questionnaire. Following the lessons learned previously about the database, the children decided to input their data straight into the computer. Although still time consuming, this was much quicker and more accurate than the collection of data by hand, and the results of the survey could instantly be sorted and interrogated.

Once the data had been entered into the computer, we were able to interrogate it using the magnifying glass icon. We looked at a dialogue box and decided what we wanted to sort. We then looked at the results both statistically and graphically. We could also ask for different conditions to be present and the computer would search and sort the records. We also produced graphs to show our results.

We used various different types of graph to show our results. We experimented with them until we got the one we wanted. We also had the opportunity to look at the results as a spreadsheet. This helped in sorting and in gaining an overview of our findings. We sorted the data in a variety of ways using the program. It was easy to do. The spreadsheet was an easy way to display the information. If we wanted to, we could use formulae to calculate different things in the spreadsheet but in our case this was inappropriate.

A spreadsheet consists of a series of boxes or cells spread out like the grid on graph paper. The usual context for a spreadsheet is financial, where costs and expenditure can be trialled and modelled. Into each cell may be placed a number, word or a formula. Spreadsheets allow pupils to see a large amount of information displayed at once. Columns and rows containing data can be sorted

Figure 6.7 Entering data on a spreadsheet

and searched as demonstrated above and data may be graphed. Values within cells may be determined by a formula. This makes spreadsheets useful as tools to predict what will happen if particular values are changed. There are many spreadsheets for educational use, some appropriate for Key Stage 1, where the minimum of spreadsheet facilities are available. As pupils develop in both IT and mathematical skills then a more sophisticated spreadsheet should be used. This type of software offers opportunity to model a situation, by being able to change values within the spreadsheet and seeing what the effect is. This use is covered in more detail in the chapter on modelling.

The complete process of an information-handling task may be broken down into several distinct stages. The following sequence is outlined by Heather Govier (*Making Sense of Information*, NCET, 1995).

- A – starting-point
- B – engagement
- C – looking for connections
- D – asking questions
- E – looking for answers
- F – interpretation
- G – product

Boy/girl	D.O.B.	Hair colour	Eye colour	Colour
girl	26/01/1983	brown	hazel	Purple
girl	04/07/1983	blonde	blue	Purple
boy	21/07/1983	blonde	hazel	Blue
girl	07/11/1982	blonde	blue	Blue
girl	15/03/1983	brown	blue	Green
boy	08/03/1983	brown	brown	Blue
boy	31/08/8313	black	brown	Blue

PinPoint: OurClass
Showing: 11 sheets of: 11
Sorted by: (No order).

Figure 6.8a
Spreadsheet on screen

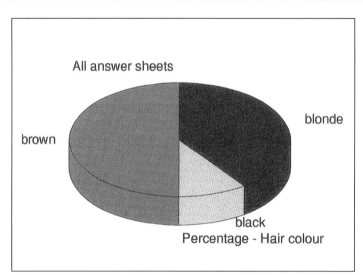

All answer sheets

Percentage - Hair colour

Figure 6.8b
A pie-chart of the data

All too often the classroom activity ends at point C – looking for connections. Govier's NCET research into the development of higher-order information-handling skills is exciting work and clarifies this complex process (Figures 6.9–6.12).

There is a wide developing interest in CD-ROM technology. Software houses are investing highly in this area. Merely a method of data storage, CDs are capable of storing vast amounts of data. Whereas a normal floppy disk will typically hold up to a megabyte of information, a CD-ROM holds up to 640 megabytes. Computer systems that contain CD-ROM capability are often known as multi-media systems, because the CDs contain graphics and sound as

Figure 6.9 CD Toolbox: exploring nature

Figure 6.10 Read the text, look at the picture, listen to the commentary and watch the video

well as text. As a reference source, CD-ROM is unsurpassed. The technology for compression on CDs is improving, so in the not-too-distant future this storage capacity may well increase a hundredfold. The volume and acccessibility of information is difficult for us to comprehend. Already powerful compression techniques allow feature films to be stored onto CD, and the entire *Encyclopedia Britannica* is now available on a single CD – all 44 million words of it.

Schools are beginning to add multi-media systems to their hardware. The government has invested funding to install CD-ROM systems in schools in order to pilot their use. The availability of CD-ROM material for primary schools is increasing dramatically with many software companies rushing to produce educational material.

Two such CD encyclopaedias are the American *Grolier* with 9 million words and 631 megabytes and *Encarta* taking up 606 megabytes. The CD versions are cheaper than the books by half (not taking the hardware into consideration) but of course, in true information technology style, are able to be referenced at great speed. Pupils can access, cross reference, collate and extract details with much greater efficiency than using the paper volumes. *Encarta* contains 8000 images, 23,000 articles and more than eight hours of sound clips. The Grolier version contains 33,000 articles and 90 video clips. The retrieval software is friendly in both cases, and the *Grolier* CD makes use of the logical search mentioned earlier in this chapter. Both CDs use a timeline feature where pupils may access information. *Encarta* is capable of displaying 12 strands of world history and, by slicing across the timeline through a direct link, pupils may pinpoint a particular article. Both are of American origin but have a trans-Atlantic flavour. British CDs are queuing up to gain a foothold in the educational market and they will find a lucrative opening.

These systems are used either as a centralized reference source, typically in a school library or within class to support curriculum work, enhancing greatly pupils' access to a rich source of information. Pupils will need to develop appropriate skills to access this information in an organized and structured fashion for the early CDs lack standardized ways of working. Part of the pilot projects in schools initiative is to point future CD developers towards a more standard and friendly method of interacting with the medium.

Pupils involved in information handling may rely on IT to support such activities in an exciting and profound manner. This aspect of the information technology programme of study lends itself to support many different areas of the whole curriculum. With the emphasis on the learning of IT skills whilst using IT in a curriculum subject, information-handling skills may be developed across a wide area. Teachers need to look carefully at their curriculum content and search out areas where information is available – be it a mathematical, scientific, environmental, geographical, or historical context. Although within the confines of the classroom such investigations are necessarily small-scale, by building on a foundation of basic understanding of the nature of information handling, pupils will enter the wider world better equipped to comprehend and exploit the ever-increasing power of information technology.

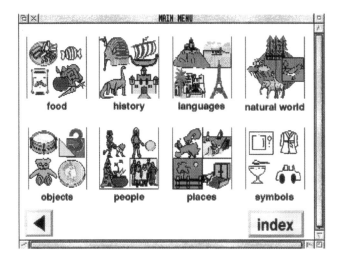

Figure 6.11 CD Treasure Chest: a key to hundreds of pictures and sounds

The kings and queens of Egypt were called pharaohs. The people in Egypt believed everything they said. Whatever they said had to be obeyed. Pharaohs led the army. People from other countries bought gold and gifts to the pharaoh.

The gifts that came from the south came overland by donkey, as camels weren't used at this time. The goods that came from the north came down the Nile by boat.

The Egyptians said that once Egypt was two separate countries. A strong pharaoh, who was the first came and made the two countries join together in about 2920 BC.

Figure 6.12 Combining a picture from Treasure Chest with information from print sources

Modelling

THE CONCEPT OF MODELLING

Much educational software at present can fit into one of two main categories. There is a large range of programs which have been designed to stimulate children's imagination and to provide them with the opportunity to experience a range of learning activities in an imaginary or simulated environment, for example, adventure games. The other types of program can be considered as tools to support and enhance a specific learning activity. This category tends to involve the standard commercial packages which include word processors, databases, spreadsheets and CAD (Computer Aided Design) programs.

An important part of the learning process is the ability to formulate a mental model to help simplify and understand a complex situation or hypothetical concept. From an early age, children construct images in their mind of how things behave. As they get older they are able to develop these images and to apply rules to predict what might happen in a new situation. For example, as children discover when playing in the bath that some toys float and some sink, they begin to build up a mental picture and are able to identify some of the controlling factors such as material, shape and density, which affect the toy's characteristics. It does not take them long to start to develop rules that they can use to predict which type of object is likely to float on water and which will sink. The development of more complex and sophisticated mental models is widely considered to be an indication of increased learning and understanding.

The use of appropriate software can help children to develop and explore their thoughts and ideas through the construction of computer models. However, it is important to recognize that computer models are only as good as the actual model used by the computer to predict what is likely to happen.

There seem to be two distinct categories of computer modelling in the National Curriculum. The first is the requirement for children to use a variety of specialist simulation software. This might involve a child co-ordinating the rescue of a capsized yacht, assuming the identity of a child living in Victorian times or being an archaeologist discovering what life was like in ancient Egypt 3500 years ago. There are a considerable number of specialist simulation software packages available, many of which have been written with the National Curriculum in mind.

The second category of modelling involves children in setting up their own models. This is obviously a more demanding task. Not only does it require specialist knowledge about the subject area concerned, but it also requires specialist knowledge of the principles on which the model they are developing is based. Some expertise of the modelling application such as a spreadsheet or a programming language is also needed.

USING ADVENTURE GAMES AND SIMULATIONS

Adventure games and simulations are examples of models which provide an imaginary or simulated environment in which a learner can explore the program's features and begin to develop an understanding of the rules which govern the model.

An adventure game involves the exploration of an imaginary environment, through which children can discover clues and rules and solve simple problems to get to the end. This form of package can be very useful for helping to develop a child's ability in determining simple strategies.

A simulation is a computer model which accurately simulates a specific situation, environment, event or process. The system governing the model can be altered, resulting in a change in response or output. A simulation should enable a person to formulate a hypothesis and test it.

A very diverse range of software is available which purports to be simulation. However, in order to address the principle of modelling using IT, it is the curricular context and the way the simulation package is used which is crucial. A useful question to ask when looking at a new piece of modelling software is 'Does the activity enable true modelling or is it a computer aided learning package which leads a child through a series of activities without giving them the opportunity to change the conditions and to observe the results?'

SPREADSHEETS

One of the most flexible modelling software packages is the spreadsheet (Figure 7.1). It is, however, probably the most under-used and misunderstood of

	A	B	C	D	E	F	G
1	School Tuck Shop						
2							
3	Item	Buying Price	Selling Price	Profit	No. Sold	Total Profit	
4	Crisps	£0.12	£0.15	£0.03	155	£4.65	
5	Chock Bar	£0.16	£0.20	£0.04	173	£6.92	
6	Cola Drink	£0.17	£0.20	£0.03	221	£6.63	
7	Lollipop	£0.03	£0.05	£0.02	87	£1.74	
8	Biscuits	£0.08	£0.12	£0.04	62	£2.48	
9	Wagon Wheels	£0.25	£0.30	£0.05	79	£3.95	
10	Apple	£0.12	£0.15	£0.03	54	£1.62	
11	Banana	£0.15	£0.18	£0.03	32	£0.96	
12	Cheese Biscuits	£0.20	£0.25	£0.05	49	£2.45	
13	Peanuts	£0.25	£0.30	£0.05	87	£4.35	
14							
15					Gross Profit	£35.75	
16							
17							
18							

Figure 7.1 Tuck shop spreadsheet

the common software packages. Many non-specialist teachers are unaware of what a spreadsheet will do and its curriculum potential. A spreadsheet is a two-dimensional framework (matrix) of text and/or numbers which are organized into rows and columns. The computer screen may show all or part of the sheet. Each location on the sheet is known as a 'cell'. When a range of numbers is entered into the cells children can then perform certain operations. For example a spreadsheet can add up all the numbers in a column or row and arrive at a total. If personal details such as age, height and weight have been entered, the spreadsheet can calculate the average values. A spreadsheet can support any form of activity which is likely to involve the organization and/or the calculation of numbers. For example, a spreadsheet could be used, by children to plan, set up and run a school tuck shop.

A suitable model could be prepared to include categories such as the range of stock items, the wholesale purchase price of each product, the sale price of goods, the number of items sold and the total money received. The effects from any alterations in cost price could then be seen immediately in the amount of profit being generated. Such an activity would enable pupils to investigate the most popular items and to consider different pricing strategies. What would be the effect of increasing the price of crisps by two pence? Would the increase in profit be offset by any reduction of sales? Would 'fun size' chocolate bars appeal to a wider range of customers than the full-sized variety and if so, how many small bars would need to be sold in order to match the profit gained from selling one full-sized bar?

One day a child was walking through the land of mystery when he saw a thing moving in the lake. There was a man with red horns.
The child said, "Who are you?"
I am called Red Horn.
The child said, "Are you friendly?"
"Yes I am".
The child said "Show me the way to the castle"
"Ok" said Red Horn.
"I can't come with you.
But I'll give you a map".
So Red horn gave the child a map.
    The End

Figure 7.2   'Red Horn takes a ducking'

A framework for modelling activities in the classroom using spreadsheets

There is a great variety of different modelling activities which can be undertaken in the classroom. Spreadsheets are ideal to enable children to work towards the higher levels of IT capability, although it is the process a child goes through which is fundamental to successful modelling taking place. The following framework suggests a process for modelling.

1. Forming a hypothesis
This is a central part of the activity. If children have not determined what they want to investigate they will not be able to decide what information is needed.

2. Gathering information
This involves designing a structure for the investigation, outlining the type of information required and collecting it.

3. Analysing the information
When all the information has been collected, the relevance of each item will need to be considered with respect to the original hypothesis.

4. Selection of appropriate information
In order for the hypothesis to be tested effectively, it is necessary to select the most appropriate categories of the collected information.

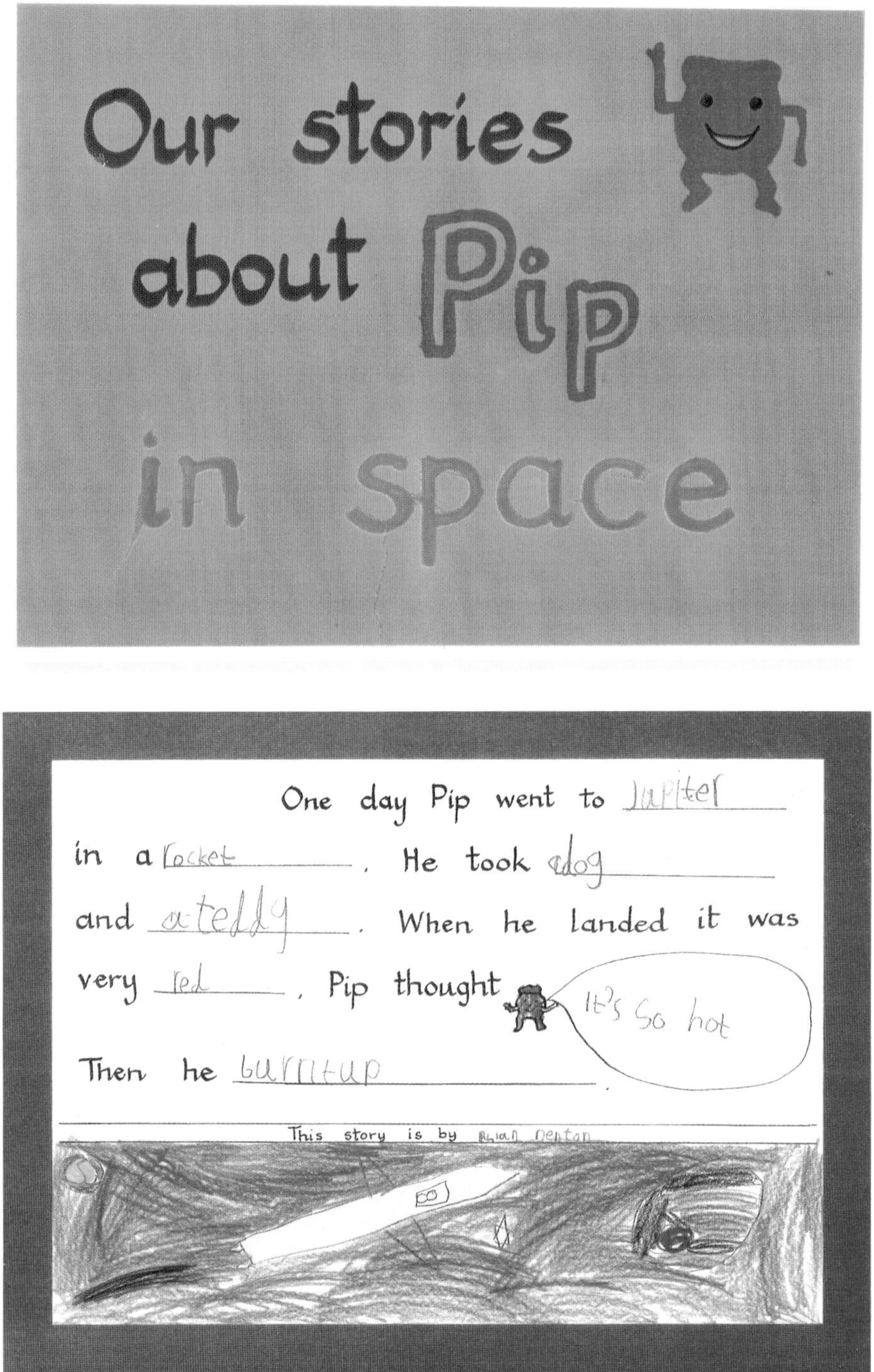

One day Pip went to Jupiter in a rocket. He took a dog and a teddy. When he landed it was very red. Pip thought It's so hot Then he burnt up

This story is by Ruian Denton

Figure 7.3 'Pip goes to the Moon'

5. Building a spreadsheet

This involves entering the data and determining if formulae are required to enable calculations to take place.

6. Testing the hypothesis

Using the features of the spreadsheet, the changes and observations made should help to reinforce or reject the hypothesis.

7. Evaluating the hypothesis

It is likely that the test results will highlight strengths and weaknesses, from which modifications and improvements could be made to the original hypothesis.

8. Revising and retesting

Further development of the spreadsheet to include modifications which can then be tested.

MODELLING WITHIN THE NATIONAL CURRICULUM FOR INFORMATION TECHNOLOGY

The publication of the revised order for information technology helps to clarify the position of modelling as an IT activity. The Programmes of Study indicate that 'Pupils should be given opportunities to use IT to explore and solve problems in the context of work across a variety of subjects.'

At Key Stage 1 children are expected to use IT-based models or simulations to explore aspects of real and imaginary situations. At Key Stage 2 pupils are required to explore the effects of changing variables in simulations and similar packages, to ask and answer questions of the 'What would happen if . . .?' type. Children at this level are also expected to recognize patterns and relationships in the results obtained from IT-based models or simulations, predicting the outcomes of different decisions that could be made.

IT ACTIVITIES TO SUPPORT MODELLING ACROSS A RANGE OF NATIONAL CURRICULUM SUBJECTS

Here are suggestions for ways that appropriate software may be used to help develop and support children's understanding of a variety of modelling processes through a range of National Curriculum subjects and classroom activities.

English

The advent of software to support the development of language and literacy for children in early years and the primary phase of their schooling has provided scope for a range of activities in which modelling can take place. The interactive nature of new multimedia packages such as talking stories, enables the combination of text with sound and graphics and this has helped children to make the connections between the way words are spelt and how they sound when spoken. The increasing popularity of talking word processors in the primary classroom has given children the opportunity to type in a short story and then listen to it being recited. Children can isolate any word which is spoken incorrectly and then see if it has been spelt incorrectly. Pupils are then in a position to model the sounds produced when the spelling is corrected.

At a higher level, there are interactive adventure games which require children to work in groups to solve problems presented by the computer. The children are able to work collaboratively to discuss the range of options open to them, to negotiate with each other to make collective decisions in order to move on to subsequent challenges and successfully complete the task. Whilst this activity provides a rich context in which modelling can easily take place, such activities can also stimulate children's use of speaking and listening through discussion, together with written tasks which might evolve from the adventure game.

Mathematics

There are a number of mathematical activities which provide opportunities for modelling in IT. The use of a programmable floor turtle or a Logo package can be used to help children develop an understanding of how movement can be controlled through a sequence of simple instructions. Whilst at first sight this might appear to be a control activity, modelling can also be incorporated. For example, children could, be shown that in the game of snooker, the rebound angle of a ball hitting the cushion will mirror the angle at which the ball approached. To use a scientific rule 'the angle of reflection is equal to the angle of incidence'. Using this rule, pupils could use Logo to investigate at which angle a cue ball would have to be struck in order for it rebound against all four cushions and pass over its original position (Figure 7.5).

Children could also be given the task of experimenting with the numerical values in a sequence of control statements which are intended to draw patterns of geometrical shapes, and to see if they can anticipate what the resulting pattern will look like. The use of spreadsheets offers much scope for assignments which employ the use of simple formulae and which may be used to demonstrate aspects of mathematical modelling.

Figure 7.4
Listening to the
text: 'How do
you spell
Mykerinus?'

THE PYRAMIDS

These are the Giza pyramids at night. The pyramids were the biggest buildings in Ancient Egypt. They were built to bury pharaohs. Inside the pyramid there is the King's Chamber, Abandoned Chamber, the Queen's Chamber and the Grand Gallery and there is a causeway outside the pyramid.

There are two kinds of pyramids, one is called straight-sided pyramid. The first straight-sided pyramid was built for King Sneferu of Dynasty IV. The other one is called step pyramid. It was designed by a court official who was called Imhotep.

On the edge of the Western Desert and west of Cairo is the Giza Plateau. There stood three colossal stone pyramids, these pyramids were built 4,500 years ago, they are Cheops, Chephren and Mykerinus. Cheops is the first pyramid built and is the biggest. It had been finished in 2565 BC. Chephren is the second pyramid, it had been finished in about 2545 BC. Mykerinus is the third pyramid it was finished in hurry so they used mud bricks to build it.

The pyramids were built by people because they didn't have machines to help them but they didn't use slaves or prisoners to do it they only used ordinary Egyptians. The Egyptians who worked were very happy because the king fed them and gave clothes to them. They had to pull stones to build a pyramid. Sometimes they had accidents, when they pulled the rope too hard, then the rope broke, and everybody fell off the pyramid.

Sometimes robbers broke into the pyramids and robbed the pharaoh's tombs when the kings' rule was weak, it was a crime punishable by death. But the tombs were so rich that the robbers could not resist.

Science

There is an increasing range of multimedia science packages which provide children with the opportunity to simulate a whole host of experiments and investigations which would not normally be possible within the confines of the primary classroom. Children are given the opportunity to form and test hypotheses covering a range of simple scientific principles. A popular activity involves the use of temperature sensors which may be used to record the cooling rate of boiling water in a range of containers made from different materials. Children are able to record their results in a spreadsheet and use the information to detect patterns and differences in the cooling rates of particular materials.

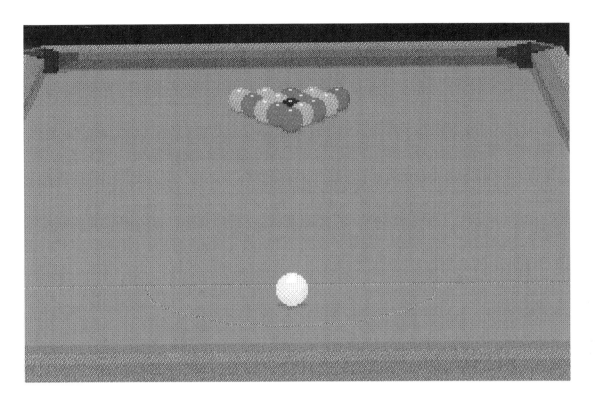

Figure 7.5 Modelling a billiard table

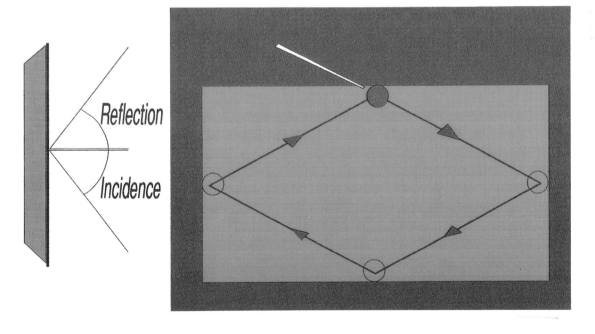

Design and technology

There is a diverse range of software applications which support modelling within design and technology. Many computer-aided design packages enable children to model the appearance of a product they have designed. The shape and size of an artefact can be modelled until the most appropriate layout has been identified. Draw-and-paint programmes can be used to produce geometric shapes, lines and curves which may then be manipulated: rotated, copied, enlarged or reduced to produce the desired result. Surface decoration can also be added to enhance the appearance. Many software packages include a tool box, which provides a selection of features to modify aspects of the screen image. Tools may be chosen to fill shapes with colour, or to adjust the hue or tint of a colour, line thickness, patterns or shading. Children are given the opportunity to consider questions such as 'What will happen to my package design if I change the yellow colour to dark blue? Will I still be able to see the writing on the packet?'

Some software titles enable children to produce 3-D forms which can be modelled on the screen. Images can be seen as wired frames or solid objects. They may be rotated, scaled or adjusted in shape and the surfaces coloured and shaded.

Specialist design software is available to enable children to produce a screen image of an interior design. They might for example design the layout of a kitchen and position appliances such as a fridge, cooker and kettle (Figure 7.6). The software will then convert the design into a three-dimensional representation. The child is then able to 'walk' through their kitchen and view the environment they have created. Aspects which they feel were badly designed, such as the room proportions, colour scheme or furniture layout, may then be modified and improved until their ultimate dream kitchen is achieved.

Other specialist software enables children to model simple electronic circuits. Schematic images of components can be connected together on the screen and a power source added. The computer will then simulate the circuit which has been constructed. This approach allows children to model their circuit designs before committing themselves to buying expensive components.

Geography

IT modelling can support several different types of activity in geography. There are a number of adventure games and simulation programmes which can support a wide range of geography-related topic work (Figures 7.8, 7.9).

A mapping package is available which allows a child to design or copy a map onto the computer screen. Contours can be added including details of height, etc. Appropriate Ordnance Survey symbols may then be selected from a graphics library. The two-dimensional representation of the map can be viewed and then converted into a three-dimensional landscape. The landscape can be viewed from any position.

History

There are many software titles which enable children to explore a simulated historical environment and investigate aspects of life during particular periods of history. Whilst such packages form a useful classroom resource and provide a rich stimulus for learning, it is important to realize that the level of modelling activity may be restricted to children being guided through a sequence of informative pages and given a series of tasks to complete. At a higher level there are some titles which feature particular historical events. Children may be given the opportunity to consider why certain events took place – for example those leading up to a famous battle – and then to hypothesize what the outcome might have been if circumstances had been different. The software will simulate the battle as it took place in history but give children the opportunity to see what would happen if they change the conditions of the event.

Art

Children are able to use software to enhance their artistic creativity through modelling their thoughts and ideas on-screen. They can experiment with a range of shapes, textures, colours and styles before choosing the most suitable method to proceed with. Paint and drawing packages will usually have an 'undo' tool which will remove the last operation if the result was disliked. This gives an artist the opportunity to consider questions such as 'What will happen if I use the air brush tool to generate a leafy texture for a tree?' This effect could be tried in the safe knowledge that the previous stage could be restored if necessary. The use of computers and other devices in art is fully discussed in Chapter 4.

Music

Music lends itself to supporting a wide range of modelling activities. Software is available which uses a computer's sound chip and can enable children to create many different types of sound and to explore ways of changing the nature of the sound. They can model sounds and investigate the effect of mixing, for example, a smooth timbre with a metallic percussive sound. With the inclusion

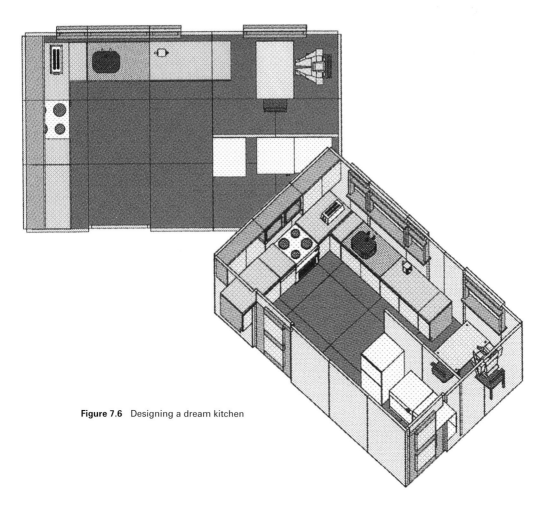

Figure 7.6 Designing a dream kitchen

Figure 7.7 'Around the world in 80 days – by balloon?'

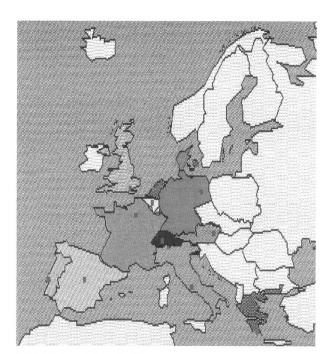

Figure 7.8a Locating Paris . . .

Figure 7.8b . . . visiting the Eiffel Tower

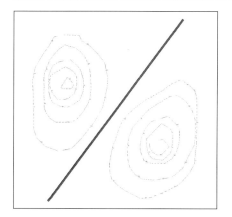

Figure 7.9a Map: road between two hills

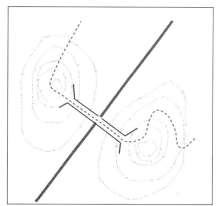

Figure 7.9b Map: bridge across the road

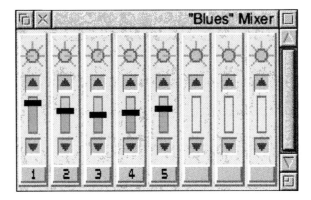

Figure 7.10 'What if we increase the bass?'

and then reproduce them in their original or an adapted form.

There are musical notation packages which enable children to write a simple tune. When a note symbol is placed against the musical stave on the screen, the note is sounded at the appropriate pitch and note length. The composition can then be played in order for the child to listen to its impact. They can then experiment in changing notes or phrases or perhaps the instrument making the sound. The whole composition can be modelled and improved before the final masterpiece in its full glory is performed to the rest of the class.

At a higher level, a musical sequencing package enables pupils to work individually or collaboratively in writing a musical composition. A child can experiment and investigate the effects of using different instrument sounds, special sound effects, rhythms and lyrics. With a gen-lock interface it is possible to view a video sequence and for children to be set the task of composing an accompanying soundtrack. Through modelling the sound and the style of the music, the children could then make judgements to establish which arrangement is best suited to the video and why. The use of IT in music is discussed more fully in Chapter 5.

NEW DEVELOPMENTS IN MODELLING SOFTWARE

The opportunity to explore imaginary or real environments on a computer screen has provided the focus for many arcade games during recent years. The leisure and entertainment industry has invested considerable sums of money to develop the ultimate 'fully interactive' adventure game. At an entertainment level, Virtual Reality (VR) is able to provide all the necessary sensory information to persuade human beings that they are part of a virtual world. Participants have been required to stand on a specialist platform, wear full facial helmets with stereo video and sound, together with a special glove which detects orientation and movement. The virtual reality software is able to detect movements of the head and body in real time and recreate these within the computerized environment. Although the resolution and detail of the graphics are still at early stages of development, the physical and sensory effect is quite stunning. It is possible to have several participants wired up simultaneously so that they can interact together in real time within the virtual environment.

There are many serious applications of virtual reality which are becoming more affordable and accessible. In medicine, VR is being developed and used to train doctors and surgeons to perform complex operations. Architects are beginning to use VR to create a three-dimensional representation of a building. The technical details of structure and appearance can be fully explored and visualized by prospective clients and financiers prior to any commitment to build being made. It is now possible to explore the Sistine Chapel in detail from a computer screen. Using a specially adapted tracker ball device, the viewer may walk through the chapel in real time electing to look at any object in detail. The quality of graphics is breathtaking. The manufacturing industry is beginning to make extensive use of VR during the research and development of a particular product. It is possible to create, develop, model and test a car on screen prior to any prototype being made. The vehicle can be walked around, sat in and viewed from any angle. The mechanical operation of items such as doors, windows and seats can be viewed at will.

The increasing speed and power of computer hardware combined with the sophistication of software is making the dream of VR a practical reality. Software is commercially available through which it is possible to create a convincing virtual world. For example, a tour of a domestic house and garden can take place, with rooms, furniture and other objects being scrutinized in real time. A compact disc can be loaded into a CD player and listened to in full stereo. Upon discovering the virtual remote control the television can be operated. It is possible to watch a current TV broadcast being displayed within the virtual world on the television. When walking around the television, the perspective of the screen and picture is faithfully reproduced.

If we are to consider the degree of technological advancement of IT during the past decade, then the potential for major developments in virtual reality over the next ten years and its place in the primary classroom of tomorrow looks very exciting.

Control and Monitoring

We enter the classroom and see two girls over in a corner stooped over a red and white Lego model. 'No, no. It's spinning before it's washing!' The little Lego washing machine is wobbling precariously on top of the class computer monitor, held in place by wires connected to a black box with flashing lights. The spinning action is part of a sequence of instructions the two girls are working on. 'We should put a repeat command in between here,' replies the other, pointing to the long list of instructions on the screen. Eventually the miniature machine calms down to a more sedate wash and spin with accompanying lights to indicate which part of the washing cycle the machine had reached. The two girls excitedly gather nearby classmates in order to demonstrate their success.

We visit a different school and as we walk along a corridor we can hear a low continuous buzzing. Approaching us some distance away down the corridor we see a grey hemisphere on wheels pulling a little buggy with cardboard cutout people aboard. Suddenly it stops, plays a little tune, turns around and heads off in the direction whence it came. This is a programmable robot going about its educational business. We glean from the small excited group of seven-year-olds that Henry, the robot, is a bus delivering his passengers to the shops. The route Henry takes, the sounds he makes and where he stops are all controlled by a sequence of key presses entered into a keypad on his casing.

So many aspects of our lives now involve the pressing of keys in a particular order – the microwave oven, the digital watch (especially twice a year when we have to change the time from BST to GMT or vice versa), using a bank card at a cash point, electronic central heating control and programming the video tape recorder – to mention a few. Hopefully we *have* control. The key-pressing sequence allows us to achieve what we want provided of course that we enter the correct sequence. Behind all these key presses lies a logic. This logic could loosely be called a language: there is a syntax, a correct way of ordering the sequence of presses.

In the two scenarios above, both groups of children were learning to use such a control language. This learning process often involves other aspects of the curriculum, especially mathematics and language. Control activities may

Figure 8.1a 'That's not far enough'

Figure 8.1b Using sequencing cards to program a Roamer

include additional computer peripherals such as the Lego Lines control box used by the girls developing their washing-machine sequence or by entering commands into a programmable robot. But early control activities may well include discussion and demonstration of everyday control equipment such as the remote unit that operates a video tape recorder.

This chapter will cover three main areas: early control activities using programmable robots; progression to the use of a control box for more complex control and monitoring activities; and using a screen turtle to extend pupils' use of a sequencing language and to develop their mathematical thinking.

Teachers should plan for progression within control activities. Firstly, at Key Stage 1, the pupil may play programming games with a friend. The friend becomes a robot and should only respond to certain commands. The programmer then asks the 'robot' to carry out a sequence of commands. The vocabulary of movement and direction is essential for such activities, and the idea of direction is important. The robot has direction; it starts by facing a particular direction and ends up pointing in another direction. This change in

direction is an indicator of the angle it has turned through. An angle is a difficult concept for a young child to grasp, but physical involvement in the robot game may well help the understanding of this concept. Also the relativity of left and right is easily demonstrated here – as you face someone your left is their right – learning to cope with this situation helps with later direction-taking commands. Gradually the confidence to build up longer and more complex sequences of instructions is developed.

From such physical floor exercises the logical progression is for pupils to program a real robot (Figure 8.1). One such robot, the Valiant Roamer, is designed to offer a wide range of command facilities for the young programmer yet is also capable of stretching the older pupils – including the adult learner. With initial simple commands such as forwards, backwards, left and right turns, the Roamer should not present too great a cerebral leap from the previous introductory floor activities for the young child.

A starting-point for progression is where pupils 'play' with a programmable robot – pupils respond positively to such a classroom addition. There are several types of robot allowing varying degrees of complexity of programming. Commands are usually entered through a keypad, or when linked to a computer the commands may be entered via the computer keyboard.

By endeavouring to get the robot to behave in a particular way pupils' minds may benefit mathematically and logically. They hopefully learn to sequence such commands in an organized fashion, trying out various strategies and recording their choices and results so that patterns within their sequences can be spotted.

What else can such a programmable robot do? Firstly the Roamer can repeat any sequence of commands. This saves greatly on key-pressing. For example, programming a Roamer to perform a square would normally consist of pressing the following keys:

f1 (*forward 1*)
ri 90 (*turn right 90°*)
f1
ri 90
f1
ri 90
f1
ri 90

but by using the repeat facility this becomes

R4 (*repeat four times*)
[f1
ri 90]

almost halving the number of key presses.

Figure 8.3 Light sensor

DELTA.

Delta is an exciting program which enables children to give the computer instructions to make designs and patterns. We use commands such as left 50,right 90,forward 80 to control a small triangle called a turtle and that would make shapes.

On Delta we had to make different shapes. We could change the colour of the turtle and we could also make patterns by using instructions. We would then be able to make our pattern.The insructions that we had to give were like:

Forward 50
Right 90
Forward 50
Right 90
Forward 50
Right 90
Forward 50
Right 90

Which would draw a square

Then we learned how to BUILD programs and use REPEAT to make patterns by doing this:

Repeat 90
Draw Square
Right 4
End

So we would end up with a pattern by rotating the square 90 times.

We like using Delta because we can make some really cool patterns.

By Sophie Pego and Gemma Wood

Figure 8.4

Figure 8.5

For Key Stage 2 users a second powerful Roamer facility is the ability to accept what are known as procedures. A procedure is a sequence of instructions that can be entered into the robot and saved for subsequent use. This set of instructions is given a unique name. Such procedures may be sequences of commands that may recur several times. The procedure, given a name, need only be entered into the robot once, and whenever that particular sequence of commands is required then entering the procedure name will initiate it. This offers pupils the opportunity to program in an organized and tidy fashion. For example if we wanted our roamer to pirouette a number of times within a longer sequence of commands it would be economical to enter the pirouette sequence as a procedure. Once entered as a procedure we could call it up anywhere within a sequence by just entering the procedure title. The Roamer's procedures are named **P1, P2 . . . P99**. So we would enter: **P1 [Ri 360]**. This means that whenever **P1** is entered the Roamer will pirouette – turn right through 360 degrees. We could make the robot perform a square with a pirouette at each corner – **R4 [P1 F1 Ri 90]**.

Another advantage of using procedures is that finding errors in the sequence is made easier. Suppose we had a series of procedures that made the Roamer go forwards, scoop up a paper cup, turn around and come back. There could be three discrete procedures, **P1** the outward journey, **P2** the scooping and turning part and **P3** the homeward journey. If the outward journey is incorrect in some way then we need only be concerned with the checking of **P1**.

The Roamer can leave a trace of its movements by having a felt pen inserted through a hole in its centre. The moves traced out can display intricate patterns, giving visual evidence of how the pupils have sequenced commands and allowing them to make corrections where necessary. Often such displays demonstrate how complex designs are made up from repeats of simpler patterns – demonstrating that complexity may result from simple patterns repeated.

At Key Stage 2, pupils progress to using a control box. The control box may have sensors attached to it so that changes in the environment may be detected. A sensor is a device which undergoes a change when particular conditions vary. For example the mercury in a clinical thermometer expands as its temperature increases. A light-sensitive device changes its electrical resistance when the light varies (Figure 8.3). A normal electrical switch changes from an electrical conductor to a non-conductor as the switch is opened and closed. Sensors such as these when connected to a control box are known as inputs – they input information into the control box. On detecting a change at the input, such as a switch going from off to on, the control box can be programmed to react in a particular way.

As well as inputs, control boxes usually have what are known as outputs. Outputs allow the control box to switch electrical current on or off. Typically components connected to outputs are motors, lights or buzzers, in fact any device that can be switched on or off. The control box may be connected to a computer and through the computer the pupil programs the control box to react in a particular way. For example a simple program may be: 'If the input changes from off to on, then switch on the buzzer and light for ten seconds.' The input in this case may be a simple pressure switch that the pupil has made in the context of alarming a model house, the outputs being a buzzer and a light. The commands which program the control box are often referred to as a control language, and these commands have to follow a particular sequence. Such a sequence of commands is not dissimilar to the control sequences the pupils use when programming a robot.

This aspect of IT is necessarily more specialist. Having to be knowledgeable about inputs and outputs and having to be adequately resourced has proved difficult for teachers, but it is now expected that Key Stage 2 pupils are introduced to the monitoring aspect of IT.

To monitor change pupils must appreciate the role of the sensor mentioned above. Examples of sensors in the wider world are plentiful. Visualize the hospital patient who is connected up to several different monitoring devices – heart beat, blood pressure, breathing rate or blood sugar level. Often the technology appears to swamp the patient. The whole process of weather forecasting is dependent on the widespread use of weather monitoring equipment, much of it remotely sited relaying measurements back by radio so that the weather trends and patterns can be forecast.

Through the use of sensing devices attached to a data collecting box, pupils at Key Stage 2 can gain experience of the monitoring function of information technology. The context may be a design and technology project (building the burglar alarm for the model house), or a scientific context (logging weather change over a period of time). The sensor devices may range from a simple on–off switch in a pressure mat, to a more sophisticated weather-monitoring station attached to the school roof.

There is a related area of control which includes sequencing instructions to produce patterns on the computer screen (Figures 8.4, 8.5). It is less demanding of resources and rich in learning opportunities. Such activities often come under the generic heading of turtle graphics or Logo. Turtle graphics are the means whereby, through the entering of simple commands in the correct sequence, patterns of varying complexity can be produced on the screen.

To produce these patterns there are several different versions of the Logo language, but all use a friendly and logical way of interacting with the computer. Commands are easily recognizable, such as 'Forward 20', 'Left 90', and through entering such sequences of commands, complex patterns may be built up on the computer screen (Figure 8.5). Similar to the patterns that the robot draws on the floor, pupils experiment and explore the possibilities. The opportunity for mathematical reasoning and trial and error is part of the Logo environment. Pupils may build procedures and construct complex patterns through the gradual piecing-together of simpler patterns – complexity may be born out of repeated simplicity.

Whatever the context of its use, pupils find Logo a rewarding activity. It may be used at a superficial level and more fully explored at later stages. The graphic results speak for themselves and demonstrate the wide variety of use of information technology.

Assessing IT

RECOGNIZING IT CAPABILITY

Thinking and doing

One of the problems of defining IT capability is the word 'technology': despite the emergence of technology as a curriculum subject, it can still conjure up images of electronic components, flashing lights and switches, which in order to operate them require an extensive range of specialist skills. Exceptionally complicated language and inaccessible vocabulary are also part of this image. There can be a tendency therefore to think of information technology capability in terms of operating machines of various kinds. Although such skills are obviously important, IT capability is essentially about *thinking*.

The National Curriculum Programmes of Study emphasize the use to which technical skills are put in problem solving and investigational activities, using words such as interpret, analyse, explore, select and classify. Whilst it is relatively straightforward to decide whether a child can load a file into an application, save and retrieve work, copy disks and so on, the assessment of thinking processes is rather more complicated. Judgements about IT capability will therefore involve both confidence and expertise in handling equipment and what might be called higher order thinking skills.

Children who are developing IT capability will become increasingly confident in these two dimensions of thinking and doing. They will be able to select and use methods which are appropriate to their task and to identify situations where the use of the computer may or may not be relevant. They will become more able to reflect and comment on their use of IT and begin to recognize how information technology affects the way in which people live and work.

Children can begin to appreciate some of the ethical issues relating to personal information being stored on computers as they are encouraged to talk about the different kinds of personal information which might be kept in different places, such as on doctors' records, at a bank or for clubs and societies, and to reflect on how this information is used. It is necessary to identify how children are progressing with these aspects of their use of IT, in addition to their skill in handling the equipment, when making an assessment of their IT capability.

THE IMPORTANCE OF ASSESSMENT

Every teacher makes certain assumptions about what the learners know. Such assumptions have traditionally been based on the year group or the class, and the work of bodies such as the Assessment of Performance Unit (APU) enabled teachers to refine their judgements. Following the publication of the report by TGAT (Task Group on Assessment and Testing) the National Curriculum also defined broad areas of knowledge which could be expected at four key stages. These developments, together with the increasing emphasis on accountability, have led to intense interest in assessment, and in the recording and reporting of results.

Teachers are generally more concerned with assessment which is formative, i.e. used to determine subsequent provision, rather than summative assessment, which is used frequently to measure the effectiveness of teachers and schools at the end of a particular year or phase. However, it is important that schools adopt procedures which fulfil both purposes; day-to-day decisions need to be taken to ensure that children are working at an appropriate level, and parents, other schools and OFSTED inspectors will demand evidence of achievement. The official framework for the inspection of IT is discussed in the following chapter.

PLANNING FOR ASSESSMENT

Ideally an assessment task should be planned at the same time as a curriculum topic which will involve the use of IT. Careful consideration should be given to how the task relates to the Programmes of Study, and this will help to determine which aspect(s) of IT are to be assessed.

Having identified opportunities for the use of IT in the planned topic, a decision will have to be made about the suitability of the activity for assessment purposes. Some tasks will not be suitable for this, and others will require some extra help to enable the teacher to concentrate on observing and making notes.

Therefore the software should be checked to confirm the particular aspects of IT capability which are likely to be demonstrated, and to ensure that the children concerned are familiar with it. Because the time individual children have using IT is limited, it is tempting to use this time for assessing their capabilities, but biased results would be obtained if children were using unfamiliar equipment or trying a particular technique for the first time.

In addition to organizing the timetable and perhaps arranging for some extra classroom assistance when carrying out a planned observation, the availability of equipment should be confirmed. Where a team of teachers share a number of computers, it may be helpful for one group of children to have access to all the equipment for a particular session, enabling the hands-on time to be maximized.

ORGANIZING FOR ASSESSMENT

Classroom organization and management are based on individual preferences and will vary from class to class and teacher to teacher. Some tend to spend more time working with the whole class; others prefer a more integrated group or individual approach. Although many of the thinking processes referred to earlier can be assessed without access to a computer – by direct discussions with children or listening in to their conversations with each other – other dimensions of IT capability obviously demand a hands-on situation. Within the constraints of a normal classroom environment some grouping of children will therefore be necessary.

For example, children at Key Stage 1 working on the topic of 'Ourselves' would typically be given a number of tasks to work on in small groups. One group might be using mirrors to draw self-portraits, another compiling their individual family trees on so on. Some children will be collecting data about themselves and their friends, and completing data collection sheets ready for entering it into a database previously prepared by the teacher. A few children may have sufficient confidence and competence to be able to structure and create the database file for themselves and be able to collect and enter data into their file. If the children are organized so that those with similar abilities and experiences are grouped together, then the latter two activities will provide opportunities to undertake assessments in handling information.

Once it has been decided which group is to be assessed, it is important that the children in other groups have all the materials and equipment available that they will need to continue with the task set without requiring any more attention. If at all possible, another adult (or child) can be given the task of helping the other groups and dealing with any difficulties which might arise.

OBSERVATION FOR ASSESSMENT

It is important to spend a few minutes explaining to the children exactly what they have to do, and ensuring that they are happy with the task and familiar with any equipment and software involved. Some time should be spent watching the interaction between the children in the group, and if possible making notes about who seems to be contributing most or least to the discussions which follow. If it is found that one particular child is dominating the conversation, intervention may be necessary to enable the other children to offer their thoughts, ideas or opinions. It is hard for a teacher to resist intervening, but if the children are talking and discussing ideas easily it is usually best to let the conversation flow and to concentrate on assessing the individual contributions.

Whilst the children are taking their turn to complete the database, comments from the other members of the group should be noted: Are they providing helpful suggestions to the person operating the keyboard? Are they pointing out where mistakes have been made in the text being entered? Are they noticing where an error has occurred either in the typing in of the data, or in understanding the on-screen commands?

When the task has been completed to the children's satisfaction, they should be encouraged to save their work, and to print out some of their notes and some of the results of their investigations. It is important to remember that these print-outs have been produced as a group effort. The print-outs alone cannot be used to indicate an individual's IT capability, but they can help in building up an impression of levels of attainment in relation to the level descriptions contained in the National Curriculum Orders.

In addition to observing and noting what happened while the group was working, a few minutes can be spent in talking to the individuals within the group about what they have done. A structured conversation is probably more useful than either a formal interview with the teacher asking a sequence of questions or a very casual discourse which might miss important issues.

Continuing with the example mentioned earlier, where the children have designed and collected data to enter into their database on 'Ourselves', it would then be useful to incorporate the following questions as naturally as possible into the conversations with individuals:

- How did your group decide on the information to collect for the database?

- Did everyone have a chance to say what they thought?

- Did you talk to other groups about what measures you were using?

- Why was it important to agree with other groups what measures to use when collecting data?

- How easy was it for you to enter your data onto the database?

- How did you manage to save your work?

- Why is this important?

- What did you decide you wanted to find out about the children by using your database?

- What did you have to do to find out this information?

- Can you think of another way you might have collected and displayed your information which wouldn't have needed a computer?

These questions are generally about the mechanics of constructing a database and the techniques for interrogating it. For many children at Key Stage 1 this will provide a clear indication of their IT capability in relation to information handling, and their responses can be used to find the most appropriate level descriptions. However, some children may have a higher level of understanding, and further questions may reveal this. The higher order information handling skills referred to in chapter 6 involve making more sophisticated interpretations relating to the inferences that can be made from the data. Thus, the following issues might also be raised in the structured conversation:

- If we were to collect data from our parallel class, do you think the results would be similar or different?

- If we looked at the same data for children in Victorian times, which information do you think would be similar and which different?

- We have collected data about shoe sizes and favourite food. Who do you think might be able to use this information?

USING THE LEVEL DESCRIPTIONS

Again, using the same example of children working on the topic 'Ourselves', the following pointers to levels at which children are working may be useful:

- If a child is observed using an overlay keyboard containing words relating to 'Ourselves' to collect information, then that child can be assigned to Level 1.

Level 1

Pupils . . . explore information held on IT systems, showing an awareness that information exists in a variety of forms

- If a child collects data from the rest of the class and enters it into the 'Ourselves' file previously prepared by the teacher, talks about why it is important to save work on the computer, demonstrates an understanding of how to do this and with some support retrieves the data at a later stage, then Level 2 is appropriate.

Level 2

Pupils . . . with some support retrieve and store work

- If a child is able to do all this and selects, say, 'number of children in family' or 'children who are over seven', then Level 3 is being achieved.

Level 3

Pupils . . . use IT to save data and to access stored information

- If the child amends and interrogates the data stored, selecting fields in pursuit of the relationship between age and hobbies and draws some conclusions from the findings, then Level 4 applies.

Level 4

Pupils . . . add to, amend and interrogate information that has been stored. They understand the need for care in framing questions when collecting, accessing and interrogating the information. Pupils interpret their findings, question plausibility and recognize that poor quality information yields unreliable results.

It should be remembered that these levels only relate to handling information, and opportunities to demonstrate capability in the other aspects of IT must be offered before an overall judgement about the level at which each child is working can be made.

The importance of individual dialogue with children cannot be emphasized too strongly, as not all children respond equally well to group work and discussions.

During one assessment activity Claire, Neil and Ruth were observed finishing entering their data onto the database they had designed. Neil was entering the data and Ruth leapt in to correct him when he made a mistake. Claire made no attempt to touch the keyboard during the session, but she offered useful advice about remembering to save the work at regular intervals. Claire was also fast to identify what search strategies were required to retrieve the information the group required to answer their queries about the children in the school.

Further discussions with Claire showed that she was the most reflective of the three group members. She had helped refine the group's thinking about what it was they wanted to find out and what information they needed to collect in order to be able to answer their queries. She also persuaded the group to have more fields than they would need for their initial investigations because they 'might want to find out other things later on'. She and Ruth needed to explain to Neil why it was important for them to agree with other groups about what standard measures they were going to use, and she also knew the value of saving work regularly in case they made a mistake when operating the program.

Claire also seemed to have the best understanding of how best to present their information using graphs and charts in order to make it easy for other children to follow.

HOW OFTEN SHOULD ASSESSMENTS BE UNDERTAKEN?

If assessment is to be formative and useful it should be carried out at regular intervals throughout a key stage, but not necessarily in such detail as outlined here. However, if a child is noticed displaying a level of capability above or below your expectations, other opportunities should be provided to demonstrate further capabilities. This is particularly important when the assessment has been carried out early in the academic year.

With cohesive curriculum planning it should be possible to include the assessment of particular IT skills at certain points during the key stage. For example a focus on shape and angles might provide opportunities to assess the children's work with a floor or screen turtle, in order to determine their achievements in the area of control and modelling. The production of a school newspaper will lead to word processing and desktop publishing and a certain amount of assessment could be included when planning such activities.

RECORDING PROGRESS

It is best to collect only the minimum evidence necessary to show that the pupil has achieved a particular level. This will cut down on the storage space required but will provide the basis for building up a portfolio of children's work which can then be transferred with the child to other classes within the school or when the child changes school.

Evidence can take a variety of forms, for example:

- two or three print-outs of a child's drawing or writing, showing developments that have taken place;

- a screen dump or file print out of work using Logo;

- a tape-recording of children in conversation with each other or with the teacher;

- photographs of children's work;

- a brief note of the child's comments or answers to questions;

- the child's own written comments on work done.

In all cases there should be a note of the context in which the activity took place, as a picture, print-out or a comment on its own will have very little meaning even after only a short time.

INVOLVING THE CHILDREN IN ASSESSMENT

The children themselves might also be used to record progress. They will not be able to make comments about their levels of understanding of course, but they can be usefully engaged in monitoring their access to equipment and software, and in recording their own progress in the technical aspects of IT. For example, a pro forma could be drawn up to provide a Record of Achievement which the children are responsible for filling in. Headings could include:

I can load an application from a floppy disk.

I did this with   : PenDown on Tuesday 7.2.95

                              : DataPlot on Friday 24.3.95

I can save my work onto my own floppy disk.

I did this when   : I was writing a poem for the class magazine and

                              saved it so I could add another verse next day

                              (1.3.95)

I can enter data into a database.

I did this when   : I put in a seagull into the Birds file on Datapick

                              (12/6/95). I counted the birds visiting the bird

                              table and made a graph using Dataplot (19/6/95)

This kind of IT diary, which also records the time children spend using the computer and other peripheral devices such as concept keyboards, floor turtles and Ion cameras, can provide a good starting-point for assessment. The format and content can be made appropriate to a particular class, perhaps using pictures and listing the particular applications which are being used during the year. This frees the teacher from the mundane task of completing checklists which, however good the original intentions, often prove unmanageable in a busy classroom. The reliability of such a procedure in providing an accurate picture depends of course on the age and attitudes of the children, but it does encourage children to be actively involved in the learning process and can have many beneficial outcomes.

Assessment need not be a daunting task, and if it is carefully planned and integrated into the curriculum, it can be a rewarding and interesting learning activity for both the teacher and the children. The information gained about individual children will be of great interest to their parents, and a knowledge of general standards can inform the school's curriculum development and provide evidence for independent inspection.

REFERENCES

Assessing IT. NCET, 1992.

Building IT Capability. NCET, 1992/93.

Getting Started with Information Handling. NCET, 1994.

National Curriculum. SCAA/HMSO, 1995.

Report of the Task Group on Assessment and Testing. HMSO, 1987.

Towards a School IT Policy

Where IT is well managed, there will be a whole school IT policy
which details practice and informs decisions. (NCET)

Given the rapidly changing nature of both the hardware and software available,
one might be forgiven for thinking that one was always working towards an IT
Policy in a school, as opposed to ever arriving at a stage where satisfaction was
guaranteed! Indeed it is probably sensible to regard the task of producing and
implementing an IT policy as one from which it is possible to take short rest
periods, but one which is never completed. Available resources in the form of
hardware, software, and staff expertise are ever changing.

IT is expensive to resource and requires considerable commitment to staff
development if it is to be effective. It is essential that headteachers, governors
and co-ordinators work together to implement an IT policy in school which
goes beyond the two or three pages of A4 which may comprise the policy
statement. Those controlling the budget must have a clear idea, and agree on,
the place of IT in the curriculum as identified in the Information Technology
orders, and also its place in supporting subject areas across the curriculum.
They need to judge the school's ability to deliver using the current equipment
and staff expertise, but they also require a vision of future provision which is
both realistic and affordable, yet in line with advances in technology in the
wider environment.

School management needs to take the lead, and to indicate its intention to
place IT development on the agenda of overall school development. A plan of
action will need to be established based upon evidence gained from discussion,
consultation and review.

THE INITIAL AUDIT

An initial audit identifies the current state of IT development in order to provide
the basis for future planning. The number of fully equipped stations to be found in

the school, an indication of where and how they are located, together with some idea of their condition, is usually a good initial indicator of the extent to which they are being used. A simple pro forma completed by all staff describing their planned IT activities for the current term or year would indicate their perception of the ways in which IT supports the curriculum, and the extent to which the use of IT might or might not be integrated in their classrooms. Informal discussions with staff will reveal the varying amounts of experience in the school and indicate the level of confidence generally in the use of IT. If handled sensitively these exchanges can begin to highlight areas of concern or needs for future INSET. An overall idea of software in use and its location will be equally revealing, and an astute co-ordinator will gather together an immense amount of information before attempting to assess the exact stage of development the school has reached.

The National Council for Educational Technology (NCET) has produced materials relevant to the initial audit in conjunction with the National Association of Advisers for Computers in Education (NAACE). *Reviewing IT* contains much practical advice and a 'toolkit' with helpful pro formas which can enable schools to approach the audit whilst bearing in mind the OFSTED framework for inspection. This package draws on the earlier materials developed for inspectors contained in *Inspecting IT*. Particularly useful are the statements which exemplify good and less than satisfactory practice. For example, the following statements are made in respect of Management and Administration which are particularly relevant to policy-making.

> Where IT is well managed, there will be a whole-school IT policy which details practice and informs decisions. The policy will have been developed with the involvement of all staff who have an interest in the management of IT and will have the support of the governors. It will deal with a range of issues from curriculum delivery to maintenance and asset management. The policy and its ramifications will be known and understood by all teachers. Operation of the policy will be regularly monitored and the policy itself will be periodically reviewed. The school will have a negotiated plan for the development of IT embracing both the extension of its use and the consequent requirements for staff, resources and accommodation.

> Where IT is not well managed, staff will be unclear about their contribution to the development of pupils' IT capability. Equipment remains unserviceable for unacceptable periods of time. Purchasing decisions taken independently or on the spur of the moment lead to a software and hardware environment which lacks coherence within itself and with the curriculum. Negative attitudes may be prevalent amongst staff and pupils.

IDENTIFYING NEEDS AND ESTABLISHING PRIORITIES

Using the initial audit it will be possible to identify the characteristics of current practice which help to establish how far along the continuum between innovation and integration IT capability has travelled in the school. It should then be possible to prioritize, and to devise a plan of action which is needs-driven and given a high profile on School Development and staff INSET planning agendas.

It may be that extra hardware needs to be purchased, or old equipment replaced. There may be an urgent need to purchase a range of peripherals to extend the work already being done in the school. Concept keyboards, musical keyboards, control boxes and turtles extend the range of activities available, and classrooms need to be equipped adequately if full integration is to be achieved. It may be that you are in a position to supply hardware beyond the minimum and will be able to explore the purchase and deployment of additional stations, portables and notebooks, and to consider the application of CD-ROM in your school. A strategic plan for future provision should extend beyond current needs, and it is necessary for those responsible for the budget to be well-informed regarding LEA policy and the availability of support. They should be kept informed of developing trends and their implications with regard to classroom practice.

Consideration should also be given to the range of software in use, its suitability, and its contribution to continuity and progression throughout the school. It is often better to equip each classroom with a limited toolbox of software with which staff feel confident, and with which children can become familiar, than to purchase an impressive array of programs which will be used by only a few people and gather dust between audits. Programs need to be carefully selected to complement those in use in other year groups so that continuity throughout the Programme of Study is ensured and so that both staff and pupils have a clear idea of the progressions.

DEVELOPING A WHOLE-SCHOOL POLICY

During recent years the role of the curriculum co-ordinator has usually included the responsibility for developing a whole-school policy for their subject. This has presented particular challenges for those responsible for subjects which previously had not featured very strongly in the average primary school. The introduction of science as a core subject, and particularly the inclusion of technology and information technology in the primary curriculum, has meant that many teachers have had to develop their own knowledge and understanding

Figure 10.1   The co-ordinator often has to spend considerable time broadening the knowledge of colleagues

of these subjects to a greater extent than was required when developing their teaching of the more traditional subjects.

When planning a strategy for developing a policy for IT, the co-ordinator often has to spend some considerable time broadening the knowledge and understanding of colleagues, in order for them to make informed decisions about aims, content and teaching methods. The imposition of a policy, however well written and appropriate, is unlikely to result in success if the whole staff does not feel a sense of ownership.

The IT co-ordinator therefore requires a broad range of interpersonal and management skills, and also a fair degree of patience. Agreement and adoption may take a considerable time, and despite the pressures which a forthcoming OFSTED inspection may generate, rushing into print with the final document should be avoided. In this respect it is far better to be engaged in a well planned review of IT than to present inspectors with a policy document which bears little relation to practice.

SUGGESTIONS FOR THE POLICY STATEMENT

The National Curriculum Orders for IT are to a large extent 'future proofed'. There are no specific references to the types of microcomputer which should be used, and the phrase 'use a variety of IT equipment' is deliberately vague. However, if a school's individual policy statement is to be of practical use it must refer to the equipment and software currently available and, although a strategic plan for the acquisition of new resources needs to be developed, there should be clear guidelines about the way in which existing resources can be utilized. It may be useful to consider the following headings for a policy statement for IT.

Curriculum policy

Extracts from any overall policy statements which are particularly relevant to IT can provide an element of cohesion and set the context for the document.

The National Curriculum

The full text of the orders for IT is not necessary as this is readily available in the National Curriculum document. However, attention should be drawn to the cross-curricular nature of IT which is indicated both in the IT orders and in the orders for all other subjects (with the exception of PE).

IT within the existing curriculum programme

Many primary schools have evolved a rolling programme of themes through which much of the curriculum is taught during a key stage. Although there may be instances where the development of IT capability requires additional provision, it should be possible to devise schemes of work for IT which are integral to existing subject plans. Indeed the policy for IT may be regarded as a summary of the way each subject provides children with 'opportunities . . . to develop and apply their information technology capability' (Key Stages 1 and 2 of the National Curriculum).

Organization and management

A simple statement of content which matches specific programs to particular elements of the curriculum provides insufficient guidance for teachers and can result in a fragmented approach which lacks cohesion and progression. Suggestions for the organization and management of IT activities need to be included. The scarcity of computers and other equipment means that practical suggestions about the organization and management could be given: about the appropriateness of whole-class discussion centred around the computer when introducing a database program, about the management of groups when using a simulation and about the value of individual work in certain circumstances. Reference should always be made to the fact that much of the work associated with IT will be done away from the computer, and again the subject policies should provide specific examples of this.

Progression

Perhaps one of the most important functions of the policy is to ensure that children's IT capability is developed progressively through a broad and balanced programme. Almost all this capability needs to grow through the curriculum subjects and the role of the IT co-ordinator in monitoring progress is vital. As discussed in the previous chapter, individual teachers will need to use various means of assessment; the policy should identify specific opportunities for gathering evidence of attainment. For example, if the plans for a particular term involve the use of a database, then this might be a good time to focus on the assessment of information-handling skills using the level description provided by the orders. Similarly, a topic on shape may provide opportunities to determine progress in skills relating to controlling and modelling.

Although informal evidence will be gathered continuously, the inclusion of assessment at the planning stage is very valuable, and the co-ordinator has an important function as a moderator and facilitator of this process.

Resources

The location of resources should be clearly indicated together with procedures for booking if certain items are held centrally. This needs to be carefully considered in relation to curriculum planning, as it may be necessary to concentrate computer resources in one year group during a particular period; this obviously has implications elsewhere in the school. The provision of resources should be equitable and it is helpful to provide a brief rationale for the strategy adopted. For example, where the policy is to equip one area with the more sophisticated systems, a brief explanation can be given.

Evaluation and review

An outline of the plans for reviewing and evaluating the effectiveness of the policy should be given, with reference to the School Development Plan. As IT is very dependent on resources, a brief outline of the strategy for maintaining and updating equipment could also be provided. The pursuit of leading-edge hardware is beyond the means of most primary schools, so a reminder that much can be achieved with basic equipment might be beneficial here.

Figure 10.2 Displays of work can encourage the use of IT across the school

Figure 10.3 Use IT in a variety of contexts within the school

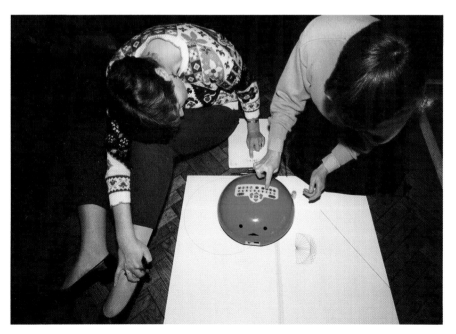

Figure 10.4 A practical workshop

FROM POLICY TO PRACTICE

Once a basic policy is agreed upon it is essential that staff are given the support, encouragement and training which will enable them to build IT into their planning, and to achieve success at an early stage.

Priority may have to be given in the early stages to improving IT capability in the staff as a whole. Are they familiar with the IT Programmes of Study and how they relate to the orders for other subjects in the curriculum? How confident are they in the use of the computer themselves? Can they troubleshoot their own hardware? Establishing what is required is often not difficult, but then long-term programmes of development should be devised to meet the needs of all staff.

Often the quickest and most effective way to begin is to organize a series of practical workshops over the course of a term addressing the issues of technical problems and classroom management. Hands-on experience increases confidence quickly and it should soon be possible to begin to explore the use of perhaps one or two applications - say word processing and data handling. If one or two programs are introduced and their uses explored with clear indications of progression, it is likely that they will be taken back to the classroom and integrated fairly quickly. Over a period of time workshops could be planned to explore controlling, modelling and monitoring in a variety of contexts using adventure programs, simulations and spreadsheets and introducing turtle graphics and various peripherals. Dealing with one aspect at a time as a whole staff and appreciating the progression through the age ranges and abilities appears to reap the fastest rewards in terms of confidence-building. Once their personal IT capability is enhanced teachers will be able to contribute to review and evaluation with more confidence, and the process of policy review can be strengthened. The planning of in-service activities is discussed further in chapter 11.

Co-ordinators need to have an overview of the topics being studied during the year within the school and should be willing to advise and support staff in the planning stages about the most appropriate use of IT within those contexts. Schemes of work will begin to emerge and through their development a spread of activities and experiences across the Programmes of Study should be achieved.

If displays of work are actively encouraged and discussed at every opportunity, an atmosphere of shared learning and pooling of ideas can be established (Figure 10.2). As confidence grows and influence spreads there will be a general feeling that the school as a whole is moving forward in a positive way in its use and appreciation of IT.

MONITORING AND EVALUATION

For an IT policy in a school to continue to be effective it has to be the subject of continued regular monitoring and review. It should be understood that agreed policy is trialled for a given period, that feedback from all will be sought and considered by a working party, and that the aim of the school is to identify and encourage good practice. For an IT co-ordinator to be truly effective sufficient time is needed to monitor work in the classrooms and to deal with the many problems which arise daily. Copies of planning sheets identifying the use of IT should be readily available together with records and evaluations of curriculum activities. Much of the day-to-day evaluation will inevitably take place informally in the staffroom over coffee, but there should be a realistic amount of time available to co-ordinators to enable them to do their job.

Consideration will need to be given to methods of observing, recording and assessing children's work in IT. Working records should be in line with school policies on Record Keeping and Assessment generally, and evidence in the form of observations and annotated hard copy retained in individual portfolios. IT work should be included in any agreement trialling which takes place between staff on a regular basis and thought given to ways of extending this form of moderation beyond the school itself to others in the local area.

The success or failure of a school's IT policy will eventually be judged on the IT capability of its pupils. They too should be involved in the evaluation of the provision in school, through constant reflection upon their work and that of others, and through their understanding of the use of IT in a variety of contexts within and outside the school. When the factors which indicate IT capability in individual children are observed to be present in the majority of the staff and children in a school, and when there is an abundance of evidence in the form of valued IT work displayed throughout the school, then it is likely that the school itself has travelled a considerable way towards implementing a successful IT policy.

REFERENCES

Inspecting IT Coventry: NCET and NAACE, 1993.
Reviewing IT Coventry: NCET, 1994.

Initial Training and Staff Development

One of the most significant changes in the management of primary schools over recent years has been the emphasis placed on staff development. There has been an almost universal acceptance of the value of a Development Plan in providing a foundation for a school's management. Priorities are established, targets are set, decisions about resources are taken and, in particular, staff development needs are identified. Where previously teachers may have attended courses largely because of their personal interest, increasingly the needs of the school as identified in the School Development Plan take priority, and funding for INSET is carefully monitored.

The introduction of the National Curriculum – especially the assessment, recording and reporting of individual progress – has of course increased the demand for in-service training, and Information Technology, as a new and unfamiliar curriculum area, brought with it particular training requirements.

CONTINUOUS DEVELOPMENT

It is now generally accepted that professional development should be a continuous process. Indeed the rate of change in education during recent years has meant that all teachers have had to update their knowledge and develop their skills simply to survive in the classroom. For example, the importance of assessment referred to above has resulted in the vast majority of teachers attending courses and developing their understanding and practical expertise in an area which previously was likely to have been restricted to a small part of the primary curriculum such as the assessment of reading progress and mathematical ability.

There have been some attempts by training institutions and LEAs to increase the continuity of development from student to newly qualified teacher; however, the fact that many students move away from the area in which their college is situated means it is very difficult to achieve a carefully structured development programme. Although the introduction of a competence-based model of teacher training may assist in this process there does not appear to be any kind of consensus about what is appropriate at each stage.

In 1989 the Trotter Report (*Information Technology in Initial Teacher Training: Report of the IT in ITT Expert Group*) made a number of recommendations which were accepted by the Department for Education. These included a suggestion that a minimum of 20 per cent of time in all elements of initial training courses should be directly related to IT. This ambitious target is unlikely to have been achieved by many institutions which have seen a vast rise in student numbers without commensurate funding. Within realistic resources however, it would seem sensible for colleges and university departments to approach the development of IT in two main ways: through the use of IT at the student's own level, within subject studies, when writing assignments and preparing teaching materials; and through the use of IT across the primary curriculum. Of course these two dimensions are not mutually exclusive; quite the opposite is true, as expertise and confidence developed in each will benefit the other.

One difficulty, however, is the number of different systems in use and their varied levels of sophistication. On the one hand students may be using a computer as part of a professional-level network, choosing applications from a menu of leading-edge software and printing their work out in seconds on a laser printer; on the other they may work in a primary classroom which has a BBC B machine and a temperamental dot-matrix printer. There is naturally a temptation for IT tutors to equip their specialist rooms with the most up-to-date hardware and software available, but unless students have access to the computers actually being used in schools, however proficient they are with the more powerful machines, they still may lack confidence when in the classroom. Until IT equipment is standardized for both commercial and educational use this dilemma will no doubt remain.

PRACTICAL SUGGESTIONS FOR PRE-SERVICE COURSES

Agree and publish a coherent policy for IT

Undergraduate training courses are inevitably complicated, involving staff from a wide range of disciplines, and although an increasing number are probably using IT in their own work, it is vitally important that they also have a broad understanding of IT in the primary curriculum. A clear policy statement which includes very specific objectives can provide the vital cohesion across a range of quite disparate departments and disciplines. Once individual staff have an appreciation of their particular roles and responsibilities, individual training

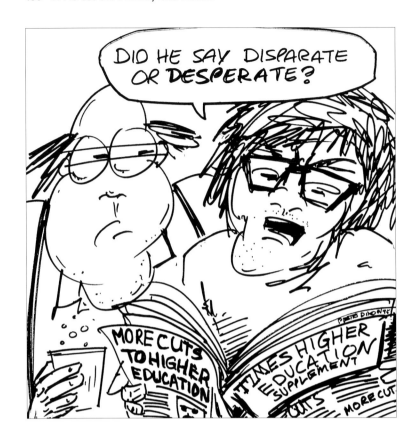

needs can be identified and a programme of in-service training and development is probably essential if coherence is to be achieved.

Decide which course will address particular aspects of IT

Students must spend around half the duration of their course studying a subject at undergraduate level, and it might be possible to agree that handling information is included in each specialist course. Typical topics might be:

English: database of book reviews
Maths: spreadsheet applications
Science: flora/fauna records
Technology: data on materials
History: use of census data
Geography: weather records
Art: manipulating screen images
Music: storing and retrieving sounds
PE: fitness/health records
RE: database of world religions

Such work could be introduced at two levels: as part of the students' own investigations and research; and within the pedagogic element of subject studies at a level appropriate to the first two key stages.

The nature of shorter courses which are designed to enable students to teach across the curriculum means that there is often insufficient time to deal effectively with IT. Although an element of direct tuition is essential, given the constraints of time it is unlikely that a continuous programme of specialist sessions could be provided throughout the course. However, it should be possible to supplement direct tuition with self-help materials. IT tutors are especially well placed to devise and produce innovative approaches to such provision. The criteria set by the Teacher Training Agency have ensured an increasing role for teachers, and the partnership model of initial training has been firmly established. Careful consideration should be given to the role schools might play in developing students' IT skills.

Establish a systematic monitoring procedure

In contrast to other undergraduate and postgraduate courses, students' initial training will involve a wide variety of tutors. There are likely to be different lecturers across the whole range of curriculum subjects and professional studies, together with teachers in schools where students undertake school experience. Thus, the monitoring of students' progress in developing expertise in IT is potentially difficult. One way forward is to introduce a self-assessment system. Students can be given a clear summary of the IT policy which states broad aims and more detailed objectives. These would include generic skills and more particular knowledge and understanding of practical approaches to the various aspects of the National Curriculum Programmes of Study.

An indication could be given of the part of the overall course which will specifically address certain issues. For example word processing might be covered in the English curriculum course, planning, record keeping and assessment of IT being largely addressed during school experience. Students start their training with such varied personal experience of IT that a flexible approach, which ensures the statutory requirements are covered whilst meeting the specific needs of individuals, is probably the most appropriate. A Record of Achievement booklet, where students assess their own progress in meeting the standards defined by the policy, is a useful way of recording and monitoring individual development.

Appoint a co-ordinator

The flexible system described above requires careful monitoring and evaluation. The appointment of a co-ordinator with a clearly defined role which may cross traditional departmental boundaries is probably essential for the success of any such programme.

Figure 11.2 A demonstration can be helpful

Ensure access to a variety of hardware including that typically found in schools

The increasing similarity of operating systems which work in a Windows environment means that the expertise and confidence gained using one system is invaluable when using another. However, the old/new dilemma referred to above is a very real one. Although the very basic machines are most likely to have been replaced in schools by those which use more standard systems, the rate of change in primary schools will almost certainly be much slower than in commerce and industry. Thus, the temptation to provide the very latest technology needs to be balanced by the need for students to become familiar with the systems they will come across in schools. For example, many computer rooms in colleges are networked. Students simply choose from a menu of educational software and proceed. This may be in marked contrast to the situation in their host classroom where there may be a single machine requiring a number of disk swops before and during operation. If there were a national strategic plan for IT in education, this problem would be reduced, as initial courses would have a more realistic view of students' longer-term needs.

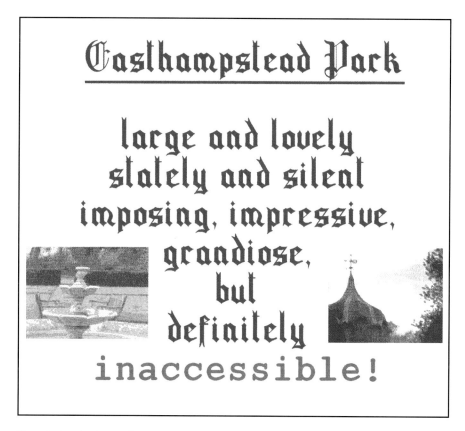

Figure 11.3   A mixture of text and graphics can often leave a novice with a feeling of personal achievement

PRACTICAL SUGGESTIONS FOR IN-SERVICE COURSES

Clarify the status of the training and for whom it is appropriate
Potential course members should be given clear details of the content; this should include key stage relevance, subject relevance if appropriate, the level of expertise or experience presumed and the hardware and software used. Additionally any expectations with respect to assignments and dissemination should be clearly stated.

Ensure the content is appropriate to staff needs
In order to ascertain individual starting-points it is essential to provide the opportunity for teachers to clarify their needs with respect to their own expertise and software familiarity. Some teachers will be unfamiliar with the many aspects of IT, and an initial demonstration of the possibilities for using IT in a range of contexts is often helpful.

Ensure teachers see the relevance of content

Teachers' time is precious and can be costly. It is imperative that they see an immediate benefit to their classroom practice. It is important therefore to make as much use as possible of hardware and software to which they already have access. Demonstrating the very latest technology could be counter-productive and demotivating in such a context.

Provide a good balance between demonstration and practical work

The old adage 'I do and I understand', is certainly applicable to developing IT capability. Teachers will come to courses with the expectation that they will have the opportunity to gain practical experience and develop their skills. On the other hand, a demonstration by the course leader can be very helpful, and pure 'discovery' methods should be avoided.

Work towards achieving positive attitudes and success

In many respects teachers are not dissimilar to children in terms of the link between self-esteem and motivation. Achievable tasks should enable them to take something tangible away from the course, so rewarding their day's efforts. A print-out with a mixture of text and graphics can often leave a novice with a feeling of personal achievement and an incentive to find out more, despite the organizational difficulties of providing every course member with a record of their own work.

Include individual tasks between sessions

If the course consists of a series of sessions, it is useful to build in the expectation that teachers will try out their recently acquired skills with their pupils. Subsequent sessions can therefore be tailored to meet individual needs and common problems. This assumes that the teacher will be fully supported on return to school in terms of access to hardware and software, and this could involve some adjustments to the normal school routine.

Exploit enthusiasm

Course members' enthusiasm will often be dampened by negative comments by a minority. This poses a problem to the course leader who needs to build on any existing enthusiasm to counteract such negative attitudes. There are parallels here with the management of a classroom where a common strategy is to exploit keenness and assuage frustration by providing small steps to success.

Ensure all equipment is working and that visual aids are of high quality

Time taken in ensuring that any hardware or software is functioning properly is always well spent. There can be few course leaders who have not suffered the embarrassment of a program failing in mid-stream. This reinforces the view that technology is not worth the investment of effort and is prone to frequent failure.

It is also important to ensure that any documentation provided is relevant and of top quality. Strong messages may be given through the use of overhead transparencies and handouts which have been produced with classroom DTP software. Conversely a hastily scribbled OHT is not only poor practice but does not give the correct impression of the potential of IT to produce resources for teaching.

Ensure adequate staffing. Co-operate with neighbouring schools

Practical courses dependent on a variety of resources are often demanding in terms of troubleshooting time. It is therefore advisable for an IT course to involve more than one tutor. In order for this to be possible courses need to be viable in terms of size, and small schools may find it more economic to combine with neighbouring schools. Although this is generally good practice, it is especially true for IT when hardware can be pooled for courses.

Prepare generous quantity of material. Be prepared for extension activities allowing for differentiation

Even if the targeting of audience is done with care it is likely that there will be a need to provide a range of activities and materials to account for the various levels of expertise and experience. This should ensure that every course

Figure 11.5a Exploit enthusiasm

Figure 11.5b Ensure that hardware and software are functioning properly

Figure 11.6 Displays of work from other schools can provide a focus for discussion and inspiration

member benefits personally from the time they have invested in the training. Again this serves as a model for good classroom practice.

Provide an agenda and opportunities for the evaluation of the course

This is sound professional practice and provides course members with a coherent structure. If the aims and objectives are clearly stated they provide a means of reflecting on progress through the course. This should also be the basis for a formal evaluation by the course members which in turn should inform future provision.

WHICH VENUE? THE CHOICE BETWEEN SCHOOL-BASED AND CENTRE-BASED TRAINING

There are of course several positive benefits from holding courses centrally and different advantages to be gained from working with teachers in their own schools.

Advantages of centre-based courses

Hardware and software

The most obvious reason for running courses in specialist centres is the availability of hardware. Everyone involved can have valuable hands-on experience, and there will often be technical support which can be called upon if necessary.

Additional resources

Despite the point made earlier about the frustrations which can be generated by using the very latest equipment, IT centres are well placed to inform teachers of new developments and to enable them to try out things before deciding to purchase new resources for their schools.

Matching the needs of teachers

Economies of scale mean that courses can be offered which are designed to meet particular needs. Typically these range from introductory courses to those for IT co-ordinators, and will include specialist provision for subject co-ordinators, teachers with responsibilities for Special Educational Needs, etc.

A change of scene

Although they have to make a journey to a professional centre, teachers often remark that they appreciate working in a different environment. For most courses it is claimed that the informal contact with colleagues from other schools is at least as beneficial as the official programme, and although this is more difficult in a short twilight session than a more extended course, it is important to provide opportunities for social interaction whenever possible. In addition, displays of work from other schools can provide a focus for discussion and inspiration.

Advantages of school-based training

Relevance

Courses on the premises can accommodate the whole staff and can be designed with their specific needs in mind. With knowledge of the particular curriculum themes or projects, together with an indication of the capabilities of the children and expertise of the staff, courses can be very relevant and immediately useful. As software becomes more sophisticated and powerful, familiarization with a new program is probably best achieved with guidance. Much time can be wasted if individual teachers are left to their own devices to explore the possibilities of new applications. Although the cascade principle is very useful in this respect, one hour spent with an experienced specialist can be very productive. A series of school-based sessions which enable teachers to build up their confidence with a reasonably small range of 'toolbox' programs can be very effective over a relatively short period of time. In addition such school-based courses can provide opportunities to discuss policy and issues about organization and management which are directly relevant to the school.

The use of school equipment

It can be frustrating for teachers to attend courses where IT facilities are different and often superior to those available in their own schools. School-based courses should enable teachers to get the most from their existing resources. Particular pieces of new equipment can always be brought in when discussing possible future developments and when helping schools devise a long-term resource strategy.

The school environment

There may be some psychological advantages in holding courses in familiar surroundings. Teachers who are apprehensive about new technology may feel

'Welcome to the IT Centre'

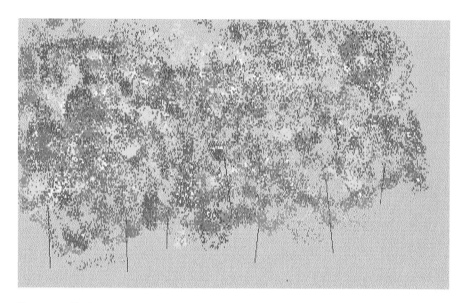

Figure 11.7 Exploring existing software using SPRAY CAN

less threatened in their own school than in a custom-built room surrounded by whirring beige or grey boxes.

Time available

Twilight sessions held in school can be longer than those to which teachers must travel and can be held within slightly more social hours. Those who have responsibilities for their own children may feel less anxious if they attend a course in their own school which finishes at 5.30pm. than if they finished at 6.00pm and had to make a longer or less familiar journey.

The extended team

Opportunities can be taken to involve the wider school team in courses. In addition to the headteacher, who might find attendance elsewhere more difficult, classroom assistants, who often are asked to support children using computers in the classroom, may be able to take part. There is little doubt that if a common understanding is shared among all participants in the process, then success is more likely to be achieved. Courses for teachers could perhaps be followed by shorter briefings for governors and parents whose understanding of the role of IT in the curriculum may be less than clear.

Trends in Educational IT

The typical classroom computer is something of a technological joke; it is frequently trolley-based, requiring an electrical point, dripping wires and cables, cumbersome and dust-gathering. Most teachers valiantly persevere with such equipment, sometimes lifting them up and down stairs or wheeling them across playgrounds to outlying temporary classrooms. Help is at hand.

Relentless trends in technology will change the picture outlined above. The breathtaking speed of development in microelectronics has been brought about by one chief factor: more and more electronic components can be fitted into a given space. Twenty years ago the computer chip had about a thousand transistors per square millimetre on it, a chip of the same size can now contain ten thousand transistors. As the transistor is the main building block of all

Figure 12.1 'Look! Control–S and I've saved it'

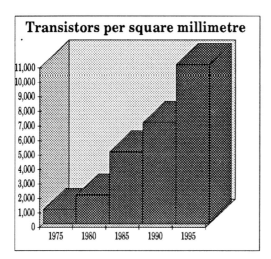

Figure 12.2

computers this trend has had great impact on both computer design and capability.

The increase in density of electronic components has allowed the development of computers that are smaller and faster-working, have larger memories, an ability to use many colours and greater potential for linking up with other types of machine such as modems, faxes and video cameras. The reduction in physical size has come about not only through putting more transistors onto a single silicon chip but the increased practicalities of merging many discrete areas of computer circuitry into a single chip.

Look inside a computer that is ten years old and you would find many chips soldered onto the circuit board; look inside a recent machine and only a handful of chips will be visible. These may well be larger as they are doing the work of several tens of the old style chips. With such a reduction in physical space required to house the components that make up the computer, the laptop computer is now a common sight, but the diminution in size does not stop there. The palmtop computer offers almost as much power as a laptop and yet is truly pocket-sized, typically being the size of a pocket calculator. Nor should the shrinking stop there. The wrist-sized machine will be with us in a short time.

However, there are limiting factors, brought about mainly by the physical dimensions of the computer operator. The size of our fingers is one factor. A criticism of the laptop and especially palmtop computer is the difficulty of accessing the keyboard successfully; our fingers may get in the way of each other. Children may well be more comfortable at using such small keyboards compared with adults. It would be impractical to have a keyboard on a wrist-sized machine! Electronic engineers have begun to harness the human voice as a means of communicating with the computer. Voice activation is already in use in 'hands off' voice-activated mobile phones and sound-activated alarm clocks.

'The lap top computer is now a common sight'

This manner of interacting with the machine would solve the finger-size problem. However, our voice patterns are unique, and such a system needs to take into account factors such as voice change when we are tired, stressed or out of breath, and differing accents and languages. Electronic recognition of handwriting is another method of communicating with the computer. The PDA

Figure 12.3 Have we already entered beech and sycamore?'

(Personal Digital Administrator) relies on its ability to recognize the user's handwriting as they write with a stylus on the screen.

Small computers necessarily have small screens attached to them. The development of small flat screens has been something of an uphill struggle. The liquid crystal screen has been the technology that has come to the forefront. Coloured LCD screens are still expensive but, as has been demonstrated many times in the past, components that are originally expensive become cheaper on mass production. The days of efficient, cheaper colour LCD screens are not far away. For not only the computer industry is interested in such developments but also the television industry. The common TV screen and computer monitor screen is bulky and requires high voltages to operate. The LCD screen requires

Figure 12.4
'Here, I'll show
you a quicker
way'

a low voltage and could be flat as a picture. The TV or computer screen of the future may well consist of a 'picture frame' a few centimetres thick.

A further development in the portable computer is the clever use of power-saving circuitry. These smaller battery-powered machines will go into electronic hibernation when not used after a short period of time – thirty seconds or so. This saves battery power. As soon as a key is pressed the computer will jump back into full power mode. However, with rechargeable batteries, battery time is not much more than three hours for a typical laptop. Rechargeable batteries are also heavy. The palmtops, however, are less demanding of power, and two standard alkali batteries will typically give over 60 hours of use. This demand for less power is because of the method of data storage. The laptop may well have a hard disk inside which, when running, uses up power. The palmtop uses a different kind of memory for data storage with no moving parts and so takes much less power to operate.

Accompanying the trend in miniaturization is a lowering of cost with respect to computing power. A typical desktop computer found in offices, schools or laboratories and costing in the order of £1000, would fifteen years ago have filled a room and cost over ten times as much. The accelerating trend in microelectronic development has meant that the computer user has got increasingly better value for money; there is no reason to suggest this trend will diminish.

The latest palmtop, with a small hardware addition, has the capability to send faxes. In an arena where the cellular phone, fax, computer and CD-ROM technology all use the same basic building blocks and mode of operation, why not put them all together? What could we call the electronic gizmo that allowed us to talk to anyone around the world, send off fax messages, search a CD and run all the usual software packages? It must surely happen in the near future, and hopefully we are educating and preparing our pupils to cope with and direct their own futures.

Such radical changes in computer design and capability will have a dramatic effect on the way IT is used within the classroom. Rather than one large machine in the corner, the class may have access to several palmtops at the same time. The way IT is organized to support the curriculum will have to change to accommodate the increased flexibility of smaller machines. The portability and lack of intrusiveness the palmtop offers could mean that the development of IT capability is an easier process.

The video revolution has contributed much to our pupils' access to increased IT capability. The influence of the video image on our environment has been great. The artistic wizardry that is obtained from the interplay of computing power and video information is plain to see in both television and film images. At last the digitized images resulting from the interplay of computer and video surpass the conventional optical resolution. In turn the photographic camera with celluloid film will bow out to the digitized video still camera, no chemicals, no fuss. Already pupils are using small video still cameras where images are stored onto miniature magnetic disks, and placing these images into computers and enhancing or manipulating them. Often such images are placed into a school newsletter or multi-media presentation that allows images and text to be mixed and presented in a carrousel fashion.

A trend which also enhances our pupils' IT capability is the increasing access they have to IT through their homes. The push by hardware and software companies into the home market has been dramatic and successful especially with the multi-media machines. Parents who may have bought the complete *Encyclopedia Britannica* several years ago are now buying in multi-media systems, at a similar cost, which allow the vast range of computing possibilities, including having access to the encyclopedia on a single CD-ROM. Furthermore, if homes have the additional piece of hardware known as a modem, then the world is at their fingertips.

A modem plugs into the back of a computer, or may be an integral part of the machine, and connects the computer to the telephone line. The computer may then 'dial' through to a similar system hooked up in the next street, town, country or continent. We take for granted being able to speak to someone in Australia or anywhere on the globe. It is a small hardware step to have computers also communicating with each other through the use of a modem. There are many such e-mail systems of computer communication available offering access to databases of information, bulletin boards, chat lines and public domain software. Of course whenever the telephone link is in use there are costs involved, although often these are at a local charge rate. There are also subscription charges for becoming a member of a particular e-mail provider, and these can be high. Schools are reluctant to buy into such ongoing costs. Nevertheless, access from the home may well be the option of the future where our pupils will have access to incomprehensible amounts of information. Beamed via satellite and telephone line, such information could be obtained as a look into NASA databases, downloaded Hubble telescope pictures, checking in at the Exploratorium in San Fransisco, finding out meteorological information including weather pictures, joining computer-chatting children in Japan, or accessing the Smithsonian natural history collection. For this reason, the route whereby such large amounts of information may be accessed is known as the Information Superhighway.

The most popular system is the Internet. This system is enjoying worldwide patronage of ever-increasing proportions. It is inevitable that our pupils will be influenced by having access to such highways; neither parents nor teachers will have control over the information pupils can access through such systems. On a similar e-mail system called Usenet, the most popular accessed information has been pornographic digitized images. The policing of such a complex system is problematic. Such issues as freedom of access have to be addressed by network engineers, parents and teachers alike.

Other developments in the educational field include networking computers over distances so that pupils at home may access their school's systems. In remote parts of the country such a sophisticated electronic mail and conferencing system can benefit isolated pupils, forging an educational communication link between home and school. Such systems are in their infancy but have already been trialled.

Finally, ILS (Integrated Learning Systems) is another contender in the educational technological race. These systems are individual instructional devices. A pupil is placed at a particular learning level by the teacher, the system takes over and, as the pupil responds to the software, the system determines what to offer next. The pupil's feedback determines the route through the learning material. Such systems do little to enhance the pupil's IT capability; pilot studies of such systems have not yet produced conclusive results. A fair question we have to ask ourselves at this point – how will the role of the teacher change in the growing educational information environment? Children concentrate well when sitting at a computer: is this the way forward towards a 'virtual' teacher, the slate totally replaced by the keyboard?

By the time this book is printed, further strides in the information technology area will have been made. The National Curriculum orders for IT were written in a 'future proof' manner so that even in five years' time the programmes of study would still make sense. But writing for the future is never safe. Who knows what technological breakthrough is just around the corner? One thing is certain: information technology is here to stay.

Index

adventure games   20, 24, 88, 93, 95
and/or searches   77–9
art and design   36–60, 99
assessment   110–19

basic skills   12–15

cascading principle   13
CD–ROMs   26, 56, 72, 122
  art and design   39–40, 41
  encyclopaedias   26, 84, 149
  music   69
  players   52, 101
  technology   84, 148
classroom organization and management
    13, 56, 113
Compose   61, 63–4, 69
Compose World   63–4
computers   142–8
  choosing   48–9, 52
Concept Designer   28
concept keyboards   28, 122
control box   108–9
control languages   102–9
co-ordinators   123, 125, 129, 133–4

DART (Direct Activities Relating to the Text)
    25
databases   79–81, 149
Dearing Report   1–3, 12
design and technology   18, 96–7, 110   *see also*
    art and design
desktop publishing (DTP)   14, 32–3, 34, 137
Developing Tray   25

educational information technology   143–50
e-mail   33–4, 149
Encarta   84, 86
Encyclopedia Britannica   84, 149
English   16, 93, 95, 132,133

geography   18, 97, 97–8, 99, 132
GEST (Grant for Educational Support and
    Training)   4
Grolier   84

handwriting   34–5
hardware   9–10, 134, 137, 139
history   18, 99, 132

ILS (Integrated Learning Systems)   150
information handling   72–86, 92–3, 132–3
Information Superhighway   149
INSET   121–2, 130, 134–42
Internet   34, 149–50

Junior Pinpoint   79

Key Stages 1 and 2   6, 72–3
key–pressing sequences   102, 105
keyboards   144

LCD coloured screens   145–7
Lego   102–3
level descriptions   115–17
listening   21–24,
Logo   95, 109

Macintosh   39
MAPE (Micros and Primary Education)   4
mathematics   17, 95, 132
mechanical skills   15
MEP (Microcomputers in Eduction
    Programme)   3
MESU (Microcomputers in Education Support
    Group)   3
microelectronic developments   148
MIDI (Musical Instrument Digital Interface)   62,
    67–8
modelling   87–101
modems   149
monitoring   102–9, 129, 133
multimedia   84, 93
music   19, 61–71, 99–100
My World   21

National Association of Advisers for Computers
    in Education (NAACE)   121, 129
National Curriculum   1–3, 5, 10, 20, 37
  Programmes of Study   92, 110–1, 122, 133

NCET (National Council for Educational Technology) 3, 82, 84, 120–1, 129
networking 150
Notate 64–7

observation for assessment 113–15
OFSTED (Office for Standards in Education) 1–3, 11, 44–5, 111, 121, 123

PC Windows 39
PDA (Personal Digital Administrator) 145
Physical Education (PE) 19, 132
policy 120–9
Primary Matters (1994) 2–3, 11
printers 37, 39, 52–3
Programmes of Study 92, 110–1, 122, 133

reading 24–6
Record of Achievement booklet 133
Record of Inspection Evidence 45
Record Keeping and Assessment policy 129
recording progress 117–18, 129
Religious Education 19, 132
robots 103–8

School Development Plans 125, 130
science 16, 72, 95, 132
SEMERC (Special Educational Micro Electronics Research Centre) 25

sensor 108–9
software 5, 8–9, 20–1, 24, 37, 49, 87, 122, 139, 148
speaking and listening 20–4, 69, 95
Special Educational Needs 8, 139
spiral curriculum 11–15
spreadsheets 82, 88–90, 92
staff development 130–42

talking word processors 93
teacher training 130–42
   in–service courses 4, 134–9
   pre–service courses 131–4
teletext 33
'three wise men' report 1–3, 12
Toolbox 40, 83
turtle graphics 109

Valiant Roamer 105, 107–8
Virtual Reality (VR) 100–1
voice activation 144–5

Windows environment 10
word processing 14, 32, 93 *see also* desktop publishing
World Without Words 20–1
writers' workshop 28–9, 32
writing 27–34